20 MARCHING ORDERS
to fulfil your
Destiny

Dr. D.K.Olukoya

20 MARCHING ORDERS TO FULFIL YOUR DESTINY
© 2010 DR. D. K. OLUKOYA
ISBN 978-978-8424-11-6
JUNE 2010

Published by:
Mountain of Fire and Miracles Ministries Press
13, Olasimbo Street, Onike, Yaba, Lagos.

All Scripture quotation is from the King James Version of the Bible

CONTENTS

Titles   **Page**

20 MARCHING ORDERS

to fulfil your *Destiny*

DESTINY MARCHING ORDERS

YOU MUST MOVE FROM FAILURE TO LEARNING

The first marching order that can catapult your destiny is that you must learn to move from failure to learning. When you learn, you are able to turn failure to a ladder of success.

There are lots of experiences in the field of destiny. What you should learn is that failure is not final. Failure can be recycled and made into a raw material for success. No destiny can be regarded as a failure as long as there is the willingness to learn.

Most of the world-class scientists and inventors are men and women who have been able to build on the rubbles of past failures. You must move from failure to learning.

You must march from failure to learning. Every man or woman who will not learn or who is unteachable is a student in the school of failure. Life is a very big school and there are plenty of things to learn. God Himself has a practice of passing His people through school. Some people call the school wilderness experience. Any man or woman who stops learning is already dead.

Declare this:
I must go from failure to learning. No one is too big or too old to learn. You must go from regret of the past to a vision of the future. One aspect of human life in which the enemy has worked so hard is focus. It is the central point and the centre of interest. Focus is what you pay close and undivided attention to. It is your vision, your purpose and direction. It is your dedication to God's purpose and vision. If you do not have a focus in life you can never fulfil your destiny. You are not called to do everything, but something. If as a believer you fail to stand for something, you will fall for everything. Focus is the door to your breakthrough. It will give focus to others. The world will stand aside and let him pass, who knows where he is going. If you keep looking at the back, you will lose your focus. The person without focus is digging his own grave and hiding the spade.

Focus will keep you. It will challenge and motivate you.

Section TWO

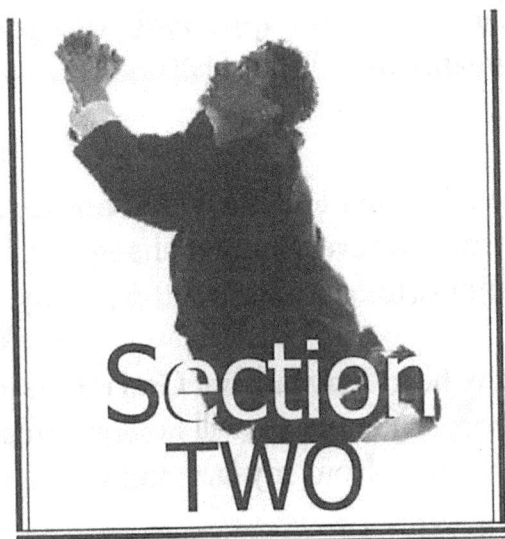

DESTINY CONFESSIONS

Today I put down my feet on what the blood of Jesus has done.

I am the manifestation, the product and the result of God's word. God has spoken into my life and I have become the manifest presence of Jehovah God on earth. I expressly manifest everything the word of God says; I am filled with the word of life.

I am not an image of failure and I am not fashioned after the likeness of a god of the tail; but after the likeness of the God who is the head of all things made. I am the salt of the earth.

Inside me is the very excellence of the power of God. God has put the virtue of His power in earthen vessels. This power is in me. My appearance is as the appearance of a horse. So, I leap and I run like mighty men. When I fall upon the sword, it cannot hurt me.

My God is the Almighty and He is God forever and ever. He would redeem me from every curse of the enemy, from sickness, poverty, barrenness, unfruitfulness and depravity.

My flesh and my heart may fail, but God is the strength of my heart, and my portion forever. He will swallow up death in victory and wipe away all tears from my face; and any rebuke upon my life shall He take away.

By natural heritage I was dead in trespasses, for I was brought forth in iniquity and conceived in sin in my mother's womb; and according to the law, I was preserved for the wrath of God that was to be revealed upon the children of disobedience. But now I am God's handiwork, recreated in Christ Jesus, born anew that I may do those good works which God had already predestined for me.

Henceforth, let no ancestral or evil family spirit have any hold on my affairs and me. Let them not have any entry point into my life; for now, I bear in my body the marks of the Lamb of God who paid the price for my life and bought me to belong to Himself eternally, in Jesus' name. Amen.

Section
THREE

DESTINY SCRIPTURES

Arise, shine; for thy light is come, and the glory of the LORD is risen upon thee. For, behold, the darkness shall cover the earth, and gross darkness the people: but the LORD shall arise upon thee, and his glory shall be seen upon thee. And the Gentiles shall come to thy light, and kings to the brightness of thy rising. Lift up thine eyes round about, and see: all they gather themselves together, they come to thee: thy sons shall come from far, and thy daughters shall be nursed at thy side. Then thou shalt see, and flow together, and thine heart shall fear, and be enlarged; because the abundance of the sea shall be converted unto thee, the forces of the Gentiles shall come unto thee. The multitude of camels shall cover thee, the dromedaries of Midian and Ephah; all they from Sheba shall come: they shall bring gold and incense; and they shall shew forth the praises of the LORD. Isaiah 60:1-6.

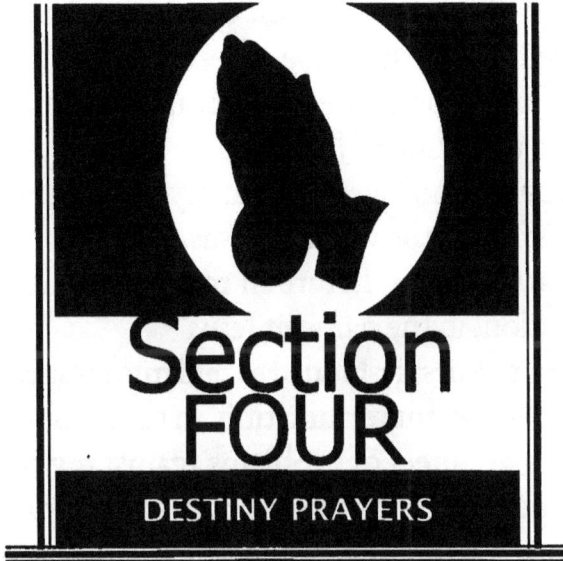

Section FOUR

DESTINY PRAYERS

Day 1

1. Let all anti-breakthrough designs against my life shatter to irreparable pieces, in the name of Jesus.
2. I paralyse all satanic antagonism against my destiny right from the womb, in the name of Jesus.
3. I trample upon every enemy of my advancement and I unseat all evil powers sitting on my promotions, in the name of Jesus.
4. Lord, enlarge my coast beyond my wildest dreams, in the name of Jesus.
5. I claim back all my goods presently residing in wrong hands, in the name of Jesus.

6. Lord, uproot from my life the evil things that are against my advancement, in the name of Jesus.
7. Lord, plant into my life good things -that will advance my cause, in the name of Jesus.
8. Let every spiritual weakness in my life, receive permanent termination, in the name of Jesus.
9. Let every financial failure in my life, receive permanent termination, in the name of Jesus
10. Let every sickness fashioned to pull my advancement down, receive permanent termination, in the name of Jesus.
11. Let every architect of problems against my advancement, receive permanent termination, in the name of Jesus.
12. I refuse, to reap any satanic harvest in any area of my life, in the name of Jesus.
13. I paralyse all spiritual wolves working against my life, in the name of Jesus.
14. Whatever hinders me from greatness, begin to give way now, in the name of Jesus.
15. Every imprisoned and buried potentials, come forth now, in the name of Jesus.

Day 2

1. I command, all unfriendly helpers in every area of my life to depart, in the name of Jesus.
2. I render null and void, the effect of any interaction with satanic agents moving around as ordinary men or women, in the name of Jesus.
3. I bind, every strongman having my goods in his possession, in the name of Jesus.
4. I break the curse of automatic failure working in any department of my life, in the name of Jesus.
5. Let the anointing to excel and prosper, fall mightily upon every department of my life, in the name of Jesus.
6. Let every anti-progress altar, fashioned against me, be destroyed with the fire of God, in the name of Jesus.
7. I withdraw my benefits from the hands of the oppressors, in the name of Jesus.
8. Let every power chasing blessings away from me, be paralysed, in the name of Jesus.
9. Let the enemy, begin to vomit every good thing he has eaten up in my life, in the name of Jesus.
10. Lord, give me the power, to overcome every obstacle to my breakthroughs, in the name of Jesus.
11. I break all curses of leaking blessings, in the name of Jesus.
12. I clear my goods from the warehouse of the strongman, in the name of Jesus.

13. I frustrate and disappoint every instrument of the enemy fashioned against my advancement, in the name of Jesus.

14. I take authority over every satanic attack on my advancement, in the name of Jesus.

15. Let every opposition to my breakthroughs crash into pieces, in the name of Jesus. .

16. I render all evil attacks against my advancement impotent, in the name of Jesus.

17. I stand against, every faith destroyer in my life, in the name of Jesus.

18. I bulldoze my way into breakthroughs this month, in the name of Jesus.

19. Thank God for answering your prayers.

Day 3

1. I draw upon heavenly resources today, in the name of Jesus.
2. Lord, enable me to become the person you created me to be.
3. I surrender myself completely in every area of my life, in the name of Jesus.
4. I stand against every satanic operation hindering my prayers, in the name of Jesus.
5. Satan, I refuse your involvement in my prayer life, in Jesus' name.
6. Satan, I command you to leave my presence with all your demons, in the name of Jesus.
7. I bring the blood of the Lord Jesus Christ between me and you Satan.
8. Father Lord, open my eyes to see how great you are, in the name of Jesus.
9. I declare that Satan and his wicked spirits are under my feet, in the name of Jesus.
10. I claim the victory of the cross for my life today, in Jesus' name.
11. Every satanic foothold in my life, be dismantled by fire, in the name of Jesus.
12. I put off all forms of weakness, in the name of Jesus.
13. Lord Jesus, come into my life by fire. Break down every idol, and cast out every foe.

14. Every wicked spirit planning to rob me of the will of God, fall down and die, in the name of Jesus.

15. I tear down the stronghold of Satan against my life, in the name of Jesus.

16. I smash every plan of Satan formed against me, in Jesus' name.

17. I smash, the stronghold of Satan, formed against my body, in the name of Jesus.

18. Lord, let me be the king of those that would please you.

19. Holy Spirit, bring all the works of resurrection and Pentecost into my life today, in the name of Jesus.

20. Every witchcraft power, I cast you into outer darkness, in the name of Jesus.

21. I confound every stubborn pursuer, in the name of Jesus.

22. I bring every power cursing my destiny into in effectiveness, in the name of Jesus.

Day 4

1. Every evil contract working against my life, be re-written by the blood of Jesus.
2. I reverse every satanic calendar for my life, in the name of Jesus.
3. Anything my ancestors have done to pollute my life, be dismantled now, in the name of Jesus.
4. I refuse to be in the right place at the wrong time, in Jesus' name.
5. I bind every negative energy in the air, water and ground working against me, in the name of Jesus.
6. Anything from the kingdom of darkness that has made it its business to hinder me, I single you out right now and bind you, in the name .of Jesus.
7. Be bound with chains that cannot be broken, in the name of Jesus.
8. I strip off all your spiritual armour, in the name of Jesus.
9. Lose the support of other evil powers, in the name of Jesus.
10. Do not involve yourself with me again, in the name of Jesus.
11. Lord Jesus, I thank you for the victory.
12. I renounce signing my name over to Satan, in Jesus' name.
13. I announce that my name is written in the Lamb's book of life, in the name of Jesus.
14. I renounce any ceremony regarding my being wedded to Satan, in the name of Jesus.

DESTINY MARCHING ORDERS

YOU MUST MOVE FROM THE REGRETS OF THE PAST TO THE VISION OF THE FUTURE

You must go from the regrets of the past to the vision of the future. The problem with victims of unfulfilled destiny is that they give up too soon. The truth is that winners never quit and quitters never win. Even if your past was glorious you may not be challenged to convert your problems to springboards for moving forward. No experience is lost. Even past regrets can become a foundation for future achievements. The past is not a final bus stop. It is only a foundation for the future.

Take a look at Bible characters who lived outstanding lives and came up with extraordinary achievements; you will discover that they came up from backgrounds that looked undesirable. Moses became the law giver and leader of millions of Jews. But he started out with experiences that were too ugly to mention. At a time, he killed someone in anger. At another time, he was busy doing what could be called menial jobs in the wilderness. Later he came across a disturbing experience when he saw a bush burning in the wilderness. He did not sit down bemoaning his fate and questioning God why he had to spend 40 long years in the wilderness.

At the end, he moved from the regrets of the past to a vision of the future. He was one man with whom God spoke mouth to mouth and face to face.

There are instances where prisoners, underdogs, avowed never-do-wells and people who failed monumentally have been known to become presidents, captains of industries and extremely wealthy men and women, who have attracted global respect.

Put the past where it belongs and move ahead. You must forget the past like Paul the Apostle and move forward.

> *If by any means I might attain unto the resurrection of the dead. Not as though I had already attained, either were already perfect: but I follow after, if that I may apprehend that for which also I am apprehended of Christ Jesus. Brethren, I count not myself to have*

apprehended: but this one thing I do, forgetting those things which are behind, and reaching forth unto those things which are before, I press toward the mark for the prize of the high calling of God in Christ Jesus. Phil 3:11-14.

The regrets of the past will fade into insignificance, if only you can come up with a vision of the future.

You must go from the regrets of the past to the vision of the future.

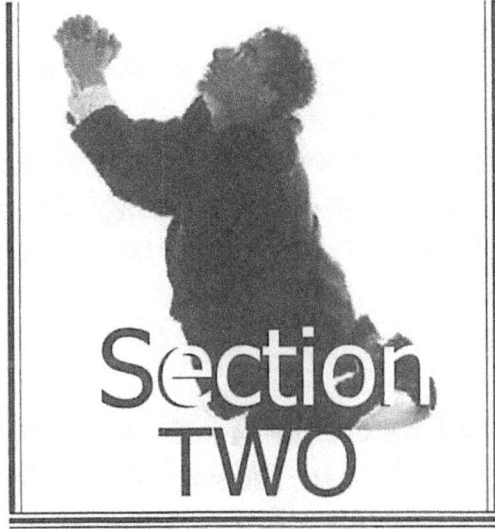

DESTINY CONFESSIONS

God is the Author and the Finisher of my destiny. He has promised to perfect that which concerns me. Therefore, I move from the regrets of the past to the vision of the future. Since the past is gone, I have resolved to forget it and look forward to a bright future. God has covered my past regrets with the blood of Jesus. He has given me a glorious vision of the future. I refuse to live in the past. It has passed. God has promised to do a new thing. Now, I shall know it. He shall make rivers to spring up in the wilderness. He shall turn my desert to an oasis. He shall convert my mistakes to testimonies.

Zech 10:6 says:

And I will strengthen the house of Judah, and I will save the house of Joseph, and I will bring them again to place them; for I have mercy upon them: and they shall be as though I had not cast them off: for I am the LORD their God, and will hear them

Isa 65:23 says:

They shall not labour in vain, nor bring forth for trouble; for they are the seed of the blessed of the LORD, and their offspring with them.

I am the workmanship of God, anointed with the oil of gladness. Jesus Christ has made me rich because He has given me all things pertaining to life. This includes profitable living and fruitfulness in all that I do. The word of God says that He will restore to me the years that the locust, the cankerworm the caterpillar and the palmerworm hath eaten..

The great army of God is beside me. I shall eat in plenty and be satisfied, and praise the name of the Lord my God, who hath dealt wondrously with me; and I shall never be ashamed. It is also written that the Lord will open rivers in dry places, and fountains in the midst of the valleys: He will make the wilderness a pool of water, and the dry land, springs of water.

He will plant in the wilderness, the cedar, the shittah tree, the myrtle and the oil tree. He will set in my desert the fig tree, and the pine, and the box tree together: I will see and know and consider, and understand together, that the hand of the Lord hath done this and the Holy One of Israel has created it.

In Jesus I have redemption through His blood and I have forgiveness of sins. The Lord will open rivers in my high places, and fountains in the midst of my valleys. He will make my wilderness a pool of water and my dry land shall spring forth water in overflowing abundance. Every dry bone in my life shall He raise with the fullness of His eternal, abundant life

I reject unfruitfulness. The word of God has come forth over me. I shall accomplish its purpose in my life. I shall not be cast out, or be barren; my lot shall not suffer unregeneration or unfruitfulness. The Lord shall increase me more and more. It is written: "Thy wife shall be a fruitful vine by the sides of thine house; thy children like olive plants round about thy table. Notwithstanding, she shall be saved in child bearing. "I am of God and have overcome evil and unprofitable works. Greater is He that is in me than he that is in the world.

My coast is enlarged by the righteousness of the Lord God of Host through Christ Jesus. The garment of His grace and mercy is upon me. He has torn to shreds my garment of shame and reproach. He has set me apart for His glory. He will show me His awesomeness and His goodness. He has put gladness upon my heart and will lay me in peace and comfort, for He is my righteousness.

Section
THREE

DESTINY SCRIPTURES

And shall say, Cast ye up, cast ye up, prepare the way, take up the stumblingblock out of the way of my people. For thus saith the high and lofty One that inhabiteth eternity, whose name is Holy; I dwell in the high and holy place, with him also that is of a contrite and humble spirit, to revive the spirit of the humble, and to revive the heart of the contrite ones. For I will not contend for ever, neither will I be always wroth: for the spirit should fail before me, and the souls which I have made. For the iniquity of his covetousness was I wroth, and smote him: I hid me, and was wroth, and he went on frowardly in the way of his heart. I have seen his ways, and will heal him: I will lead him also, and restore comforts unto him and to his mourners. I create the fruit of the lips; Peace, peace to him that is far off, and to him that is near, saith the LORD; and I will heal him. Isa 57:14-19.

Sing, O barren, thou that didst not bear; break forth into singing, and cry aloud, thou that didst not travail with child: for more are the children of the desolate than the children of the married wife, saith the LORD. Enlarge the place of thy tent, and let them stretch forth the curtains of thine habitations: spare not, lengthen thy cords, and strengthen thy stakes; For thou shalt break forth on the right hand and on the left; and thy seed shall inherit the Gentiles, and make the desolate cities to be inhabited. Fear not; for thou shalt not be ashamed: neither be thou confounded; for thou shalt not be put to shame: for thou shalt forget the shame of thy youth, and shalt not remember the reproach of thy widowhood any more. For thy Maker is thine husband; the LORD of hosts is his name; and thy Redeemer the Holy One of Israel; The God of the whole earth shall he be called. For the LORD hath called thee as a woman forsaken and grieved in spirit, and a wife of youth, when thou wast refused, saith thy God. For a small moment have I forsaken thee; but with great mercies will I gather thee. In a little wrath I hid my face from thee for a moment; but with everlasting kindness will I have mercy on thee, saith the LORD thy Redeemer. For this is as the waters of Noah unto me: for as I have sworn that the waters of Noah should no more go over the earth; so have I sworn that I would not be wroth with thee, nor rebuke thee. For the mountains shall depart, and the hills be removed; but my kindness shall not depart from thee, neither shall the covenant of my peace be removed, saith the LORD that hath mercy on thee. O thou afflicted, tossed with tempest, and not comforted, behold, I will lay thy stones with fair colours, and lay thy foundations with sapphires. And I will make thy windows of agates, and thy gates of carbuncles, and all thy borders of pleasant stones. **Isa 54:1-12.**

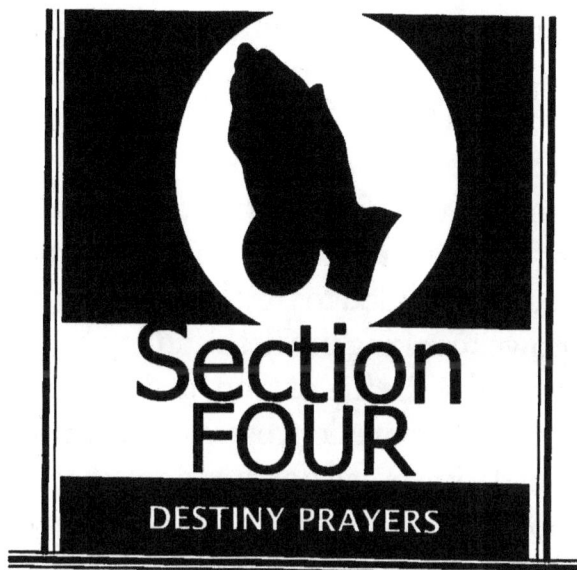

Section FOUR

DESTINY PRAYERS

Day 1

1. My place of birth will not be my caldron, in Jesus' name.
2. This city I live in will not be my caldron, in Jesus' name.
3. Every pot of darkness energised against my life, be destroyed by fire, in the name of Jesus.
4. I command every witchcraft pot using remote control against my health to be broken into pieces, in Jesus' name.
5. Every power calling my name into any caldron, fall down and die, in the name of Jesus.
6. Every caldron, making noise against me and monitoring my life, disintegrate, in the name of Jesus.
7. Every power cooking my progress in an evil pot, receive the fire of judgment, in the name of Jesus.

8. Every satanic programme emanating from the caldron of darkness, be reversed, in the name of Jesus.
9. Any evil fire fuelling any satanic programme in my life, be quenched, in the name of Jesus.
10. The counsel of the wicked against my life in this city shall not stand. I command it to perish, in Jesus' name.
11. Let the counsel of God for my life prosper, in Jesus' name.
12. Every power cooking my flesh and my health in any evil caldron, receive the fire of God, in the name of Jesus.
13. Every evil bird of satanic programme emanating from any caldron of darkness, fall down and die, in Jesus' name.
14. Every pot cooking my affairs, let the Lord rebuke you, in Jesus' name.
15. I rebuke the spell of any witchcraft pot, in Jesus' name.
16. I break every witchcraft pot over my life, in Jesus' name.
17. Let every evil pot hunt its owner, in the name of Jesus.
18. Every evil caldron or pot, be judged from heaven, in Jesus' name.
19. No evil caldron will cook up my life, in the name of Jesus.
20. Every council of witchcraft working against me will not prosper, in the name of Jesus.
21. Every agreement with Satan over my life, I cancel you now, in the name of Jesus.
22. Every astral projection against me, I frustrate you, in Jesus' name.
23. I dismantle myself and my family from every witchcraft cage and pot, in the name of Jesus.

24. Every enemy that will not let me go easily, I bring the judgment of death against you, in Jesus' name.
25. This season, my blessing will not sink, in the name of Jesus.

Day 2

1. I command all foundational strongmen attached to my life to be paralysed, in the name of Jesus.
2. Let any rod of the wicked rising up against my family line be rendered impotent for my sake, in the name of Jesus
3. I cancel all the consequences of any evil local name attached to my person, in the name of Jesus.
4. You evil foundational plantations, come out of my life with all your roots, in the name of Jesus.
5. I break and loose myself from every foot of demonic bewitchment, in the name of Jesus.
6. I release myself from every evil domination and control, in Jesus' name.
7. Let every gate opened to the enemy by my foundation be closed forever with the blood of Jesus.
8. Lord Jesus, walk back into every second of my life and deliver me where I need deliverance, heal me where I need healing, transform me where I need transformation.
9. Let every evil imagination against me wither from the source, in Jesus' name.
10. All those laughing me to scorn shall witness my testimony, in Jesus' name.
11. Let all the destructive plans of the enemies aimed at me, blow up in their faces, in Jesus' name.

12. Let my point of ridicule be converted to a source of miracles, in Jesus' name.

13. Let all powers sponsoring evil decisions against me, be disgraced, in the name of Jesus.

14. Let the stubborn strongman commissioned against me, fall down to the ground and become impotent, in Jesus' name.

15. Let the stronghold of every spirit of Korah, Dathan and Abiram militating against me, be smashed to pieces, in the name of Jesus.

16. Let every spirit of Balaam hired to curse me, fall after the order of Balaam, in the name of Jesus

17. Let every spirit of Sanballat and Tobiah planning evil against me receive the stones of fire, in the name of Jesus.

18. Let every spirit of Egypt fall after the order of Pharaoh, in Jesus' name.

19. Let every spirit of Herod be disgraced, in Jesus' name.

20. Let every spirit of Goliath receive the stones of fire, in Jesus' name

21. Let every spirit of Pharaoh fall into the Red Sea of its own creation, in the name of Jesus

22. Let all satanic manipulations aimed at changing my destiny be frustrated, in the name of Jesus.

23. Let all evil broadcasters of my goodness be silenced, in the name of Jesus.

24. Let all evil leaking bags and pockets be sealed up, in Jesus' name.

25. Let all evil monitoring eyes fashioned against me become blind, in Jesus' name.

26. Let every evil effect of any strange touch be removed from my life, in the name of Jesus.

27. I command all demonic reverse gears installed to hinder my progress to be roasted, in Jesus' name.

Day 3

1. Every influence of the evil powers of my father's house in my life, die, in the name of Jesus.
2. Every network of the evil powers of my father's house in my place of birth, scatter, in the name of Jesus.
3. Every satanic dedication speaking against me, be dismantled by the power in the blood of Jesus.
4. I vomit every food with idolatrous influence that I have eaten, in the name of Jesus.
5. Every unconscious evil internal altar, be roasted, in the name of Jesus.
6. Let the stone of hindrance constructed by the evil powers of my father's house be rolled away, in the name of Jesus.
7. The voice of foundational powers of my father's house will never speak again, in the name of Jesus.
8. Every strongman, assigned by the evil powers of my father's house against my life, die, in the name of Jesus.
9. Every satanic promissory note issued on my behalf by my ancestors, be reversed, in the name of Jesus.
10. Garments of opposition designed by the evil powers of my father's house, roast, in the name of Jesus.
11. Every satanic cloud upon my life, scatter, in the name of Jesus.
12. My glory buried by the evil powers of my father's house, come alive by fire, in the name of Jesus.

13. Thou power of strange gods legislating against my destiny, scatter, in the name of Jesus.

14. Evil powers of my father's house of my place of birth, I break your chain, in the name of Jesus.

15. I fire back arrows of my family idols, in the name of Jesus

16. Every doorway and satanic ladder to satanic invasion in my life, be abolished forever by the blood of Jesus.

17. I loose myself from curses, hexes, spells, bewitchments and evil dominations directed against me through dreams, in the name of Jesus.

18. I command you ungodly powers: release me, in the name of Jesus. Let all past satanic defeats in the dream be converted to victory, in the name of Jesus

19. Let all tests in the dreams be converted to testimonies, in Jesus' name.

20. Let all trials in the dreams be converted to triumphs, in Jesus' name.

21. Let all failures in the dreams be converted to success, in Jesus' name.

22. Let all scars in the dreams, be converted to stars, in Jesus' name.

23. Let all bondages in the dreams be converted to freedom, in Jesus' name.

24. Let all loses in the dreams be converted to gains, in Jesus' name.

25. Let all opposition in the dreams be converted to victory, in Jesus' name.

26. Let all weaknesses in the dreams be converted to strength,

in Jesus' name.

27. Let all negative things in the dreams be converted to positive things, in Jesus' name.

Day 4

1. I repent from all ancestral idol worship, in the name of Jesus.
2. Every idol of my father's house, loose your hold over my life, in the name of Jesus.
3. Every strongman of my father's house, die, in the name of Jesus.
4. I silence the evil cry of the evil powers of my father's house fashioned against me, in the name of Jesus.
5. All consequences of the worship of evil powers of my father's house in my life, I wipe you off by the blood of Jesus.
6. Holy Ghost fire, burn down all spiritual shrines of my father's house, in the name of Jesus.
7. Oppressive agenda of the evil powers of my father's house, die, in the name of Jesus.
8. Every blood speaking against my generational line, be silenced by the blood of Jesus.
9. Every evil power of my father's house speaking against my destiny, scatter, in the name of Jesus.
10. I break all ancestral covenants with the evil powers of my father's house, in the name of Jesus.
11. Every bitter water flowing in my family from the evil powers of my father's house, dry up, in the name of Jesus.
12. Any rope tying my family line to any evil power of my father's house, break, in the name of Jesus.

13. Every landlord spirit troubling my destiny, be paralysed, in the name of Jesus.

14. Every outflow of satanic family name, die, in the name of Jesus.

15. I recover every benefit stolen by the evil powers of my father's house, in the name of Jesus.

16. Where is the Lord God of Elijah? Arise, disgrace every evil power of my father's house, in the name of Jesus.

17. Every satanic priest ministering in my family, be retrenched, in the name of Jesus.

18. Arrows of affliction resulting from idolatry, loose your hold, in the name of Jesus.

19. I release myself from every infirmity introduced into my life through dreams, in the name of Jesus.

20. Let all attempts by the enemy to deceive me through dreams fail woefully, in the name of Jesus.

21. I reject every spiritual husband, wife, child, marriage, engagement, trade, pursuit, ornament, money, friend, relative, etc., in the name of Jesus.

22. Lord Jesus, wash my spiritual eyes, ears and mouth with Your blood.

23. The God who answereth by fire, answer by fire whenever any spiritual attacker comes against me.

24. Lord Jesus, replace all satanic dreams with heavenly visions and divinely inspired dreams.

25. Wonderful Lord, I reverse any defeat that I have ever suffered in the dream, in the name of Jesus.

26. Any dream that I have dreamt that is good and for God, I

receive it and those that are satanic, I reject them in the name of Jesus.

27. Every night and dream attacks and their consequences, be nullified, in Jesus' name.
28. I claim freedom from satanic and restless dreams, in Jesus' name.
29. I claim freedom from importing anxiety and shameful thoughts into my dreams, in Jesus' name.
30. I stand against dream defeats and its effects, in the name of Jesus.
31. Let all satanic designs of oppression against me in dreams and visions be frustrated, in the name of Jesus.
32. Let every demonic influence targeted at destroying my vision and ministry, receive total disappointment, in the name of Jesus.
33. Every witchcraft hand planting evil seeds in my life through dream attacks, wither and bum to ashes, in Jesus' name.
34. By the blood of Jesus, I rebuke every attacking and fearful dreams, in the name of Jesus.
35. Let the evil vision and dream in my life evaporate and condense in the camp of the enemy, in the name of Jesus.
36. Every curse of demotion in the dream in my life, be nullified by the blood of Jesus.
37. Every curse of confused and unprogressive dreams in my life, be nullified by the blood of Jesus.
38. Every curse of being harassed in the dream by familiar faces in my life, be nullified by the blood of Jesus.
39. I send the arrows or any gun shot in the dream back to the

senders, in the name of Jesus.

40. I paralyse all the night caterers and I forbid their food in my dream, in the name of Jesus.
41. All masquerdes in my dreams, pursue yourselve in Jesus' name.
42. Let all the contamination in my life through dreams, be cleansed by the blood of Jesus

DESTINY MARCHING ORDERS

HOW TO MOVE FROM BEING FRUSTRATED TO BEING FOCUSED

You must go from being frustrated to being focused. There are many experiences in life to frustrate anyone who is not focused. The road to the top is by no means strewn with roses. You may not get to the palace of your destiny by lying on the sofa of ease. Jesus, our Perfect Example had to embrace the cross in order to win the glory.

> *Let this mind be in you, which was also in Christ Jesus: Who, being in the form of God, thought it not robbery to be equal with God: But made himself of no reputation, and took upon him the form of a servant, and was made in the likeness*

of men: And being found in fashion as a man, he humbled himself, and became obedient unto death, even the death of the cross. Wherefore God also hath highly exalted him, and given him a name which is above every name: That at the name of Jesus every knee should bow, of things in heaven, and things in earth, and things under the earth. Phil 2:5-10.

Paul the Apostle also contended with lots of adversities, yet he remained focused.

I speak as concerning reproach, as though we had been weak. Howbeit whereinsoever any is bold, (I speak foolishly,) I am bold also. Are they Hebrews? so am I. Are they Israelites? so am I. Are they the seed of Abraham? so am I. Are they ministers of Christ? (I speak as a fool) I am more; in labours more abundant, in stripes above measure, in prisons more frequent, in deaths oft. Of the Jews five times received I forty stripes save one. Thrice was I beaten with rods, once was I stoned, thrice I suffered shipwreck, a night and a day I have been in the deep; In journeyings often, in perils of waters, in perils of robbers, in perils by mine own countrymen, in perils by the heathen, in perils in the city, in perils in the wilderness, in perils in the sea, in perils among false brethren; In weariness and painfulness, in watchings often, in hunger and thirst, in fastings often, in cold and nakedness. Beside those things that are without, that which cometh upon me daily, the care of all the churches. Who is weak, and I am not weak? who is offended, and I burn not? 2 Cor 11:21-29.

In spite of the tough experiences which Paul the Apostle went through, he went from being frustrated to being focused. The truth is that your destiny will only be spared attacks and troubles, if only it is ordinary. Colourful destinies will be bombarded by all kinds of attacks.

Frustration must not be allowed to derail the train of your destiny. Do not focus your attention on what you have been through. Let your focus be on where you are going. If you focus all your efforts on everything that happens on the road of destiny, you will hardly be able to look forward.

You must learn how to ignore frustrations and focus your attention on Jesus, the Author and Finisher of your faith. Past frustrations are gone with the past. The future is the only thing you have. You must not allow the past to drown it with frustration. The moment you feel frustrated you must take cognisance of the fact that your future is bright; that is why you are being attacked.

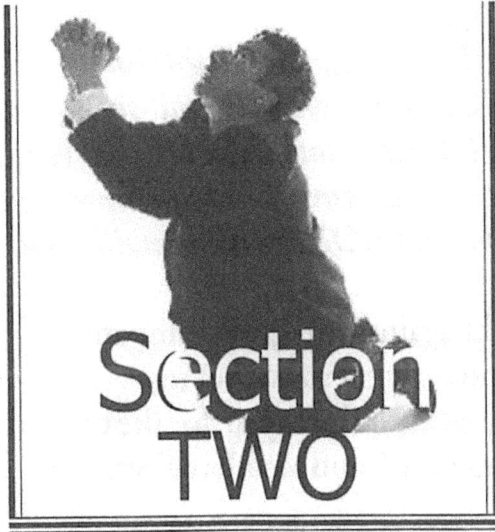

DESTINY CONFESSIONS

I am too blessed to be frustrated. The future of the Almighty has made my situation different. Hence, frustration is not my lot. Therefore, every seed of frustration in my life shall die. I am moving from frustration to divine focus. My focus is on what God has declared concerning my destiny. My frustrations belong to the past. Jesus declared, "It is finished." My tears and sorrows are gone. God has brought me out of the darkness of the night into a new dawn. A new dawn of hope. A new dawn of bright future.

2 kings 6:16 says:

> *And he answered, Fear not: for they that be with us are more than they that be with them.*

2 chron. 20:17 says:

> *Ye shall not need to fight in this battle: set yourselves, stand ye still, and see the salvation of the LORD with you, O Judah and Jerusalem: fear not, nor be dismayed; tomorrow go out against them: for the LORD will be with you.*

I have no might against this great company that comes against me, neither know I what to do: but my eyes are upon the Lord. I shall not be afraid nor dismayed, for the battle is not mine, but the Lord's. I stand still and see His deliverance.

O Lord, make for me a fenced brazen wall, so that though satan's hosts will fight against me, they shall not prevail against me, for You are with me to deliver me out of the hand of the wicked one and redeem me out of the hand of the terrible.

The Lord rebuke you, satan. I come against you, in the name of Jesus and in the power of His might. For He has made us kings and priests to rule with Him in spiritual authority, and to sit together in heavenly places, in Christ Jesus.

What I shall bind on earth shall be bound in heaven, for greater is He that is in me than he that is in the world. Therefore, I bind the strongman and cast down the principalities, powers, rulers of darkness and spiritual wickedness in high places over this situation.

I rebuke you foul spirits that are seeking to manipulate, intimidate, frustrate and destroy in this situation

I rebuke you foul spirits of..... that are operating and manifesting yourselves in the lives of ....(list the names), and all those in agreement with you. I command you to desist in your manoeuvres.

I resist you devil, and you must flee from me. I pull down strongholds; I cast down imaginations and every high thing that exalts itself against the knowledge of Christ, and I bring into captivity every thought to the obedience of Christ.

Section
THREE

DESTINY SCRIPTURES

Sing, O barren, thou that didst not bear; break forth into singing, and cry aloud, thou that didst not travail with child: for more are the children of the desolate than the children of the married wife, saith the LORD. Enlarge the place of thy tent, and let them stretch forth the curtains of thine habitations: spare not, lengthen thy cords, and strengthen thy stakes; For thou shalt break forth on the right hand and on the left; and thy seed shall inherit the Gentiles, and make the desolate cities to be inhabited. Fear not; for thou shalt not be ashamed: neither be thou confounded; for thou shalt not be put to shame:

for thou shalt forget the shame of thy youth, and shalt not remember the reproach of thy widowhood any more. For thy Maker is thine husband; the LORD of hosts is his name; and thy Redeemer the Holy One of Israel; The God of the whole earth shall he be called. For the LORD hath called thee as a woman forsaken and grieved in spirit, and a wife of youth, when thou wast refused, saith thy God. For a small moment have I forsaken thee; but with great mercies will I gather thee. In a little wrath I hid my face from thee for a moment; but with everlasting kindness will I have mercy on thee, saith the LORD thy Redeemer. For this is as the waters of Noah unto me: for as I have sworn that the waters of Noah should no more go over the earth; so have I sworn that I would not be wroth with thee, nor rebuke thee. For the mountains shall depart, and the hills be removed; but my kindness shall not depart from thee, neither shall the covenant of my peace be removed, saith the LORD that hath mercy on thee. O thou afflicted, tossed with tempest, and not comforted, behold, I will lay thy stones with fair colours, and lay thy foundations with sapphires. And I will make thy windows of agates, and thy gates of carbuncles, and all thy borders of pleasant stones. Isa 54:1-12.

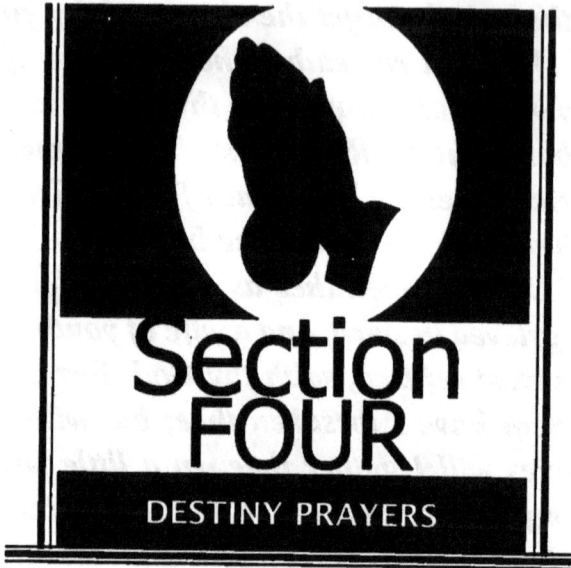

Section FOUR

DESTINY PRAYERS

Day 1

1. I release myself from the grip of the spirit of self-destruction, in the name of Jesus.
2. Power of the oppressor, release my spirit man, in Jesus' name.
3. My life, glorify the name of the Lord, in the name of Jesus.
4. I will not terminate my own destiny, in the name of Jesus.
5. Every power encouraging me to end my life, die, in Jesus' name.
6. I bind and cast out every spirit of discouragement, in Jesus' name.
7. God, arise and fight my battle for me, in Jesus' name.
8. I release myself from every generational, suicidal tendency, in the name of Jesus.

9. My Father, remove me from the cage of low esteem, in the name of Jesus. .
10. I shall not give up, my problem shall give up, in Jesus' name.
11. I bind every evil voice speaking destruction to my life, in the name of Jesus.
12. Every strongman behind suicide, I bind and pull you down, in the name of Jesus.
13. My Father, deliver me from hearing strange voices, in Jesus' name.
14. Power of sudden death, loose your hold upon my life, in the name of Jesus.
15. Spirit of the living God, arise and pursue my pursuers, in the name of Jesus.
16. I move from strength to strength by the power of God, in the name of Jesus.
17. My enemies shall not laugh last over my life, in Jesus' name.
18. I reject every internal pressure to end my life, in Jesus' name.
19. Let every internal warfare be quenched, in Jesus' name.
20. My life is not for sale, in the name of Jesus. .
21. Every witchcraft agenda for my life, die, in Jesus' name.

Day 2

1. Father, I confess that in the past I was unforgiving I harboured bitterness and resentment in my heart against certain people who hurt or disappointed me.
2. I now recognise this as a sin and confess it as a sin, for You say in your Word that if we confess our sins You are faithful and just to forgive us our sins and to cleanse us of all unrighteousness. (I John 1:9).
3. I now forgive the following people that I remember, who had hurt or disappointed me. (*Mention the names of those who come to your mind.*) I now freely forgive all these people and ask You to bless them if they are still living.
4. I also forgive myself for all my faults and failures, for You have freely forgiven me.
5. Thank You Father for freedom from the load of unforgiveness, bitterness and resentment, in Jesus' name.
6. Father, I confess to You that in the past, through ignorance, curiosity or wilfulness, I performed certain sinful acts. I now recognise these as sin and confess them as sin, and ask for forgiveness, in Jesus' name.
7. Specifically, I do confess as sin and renounce all contacts which I have had with the following occult things: (mention everything in the occult, which you have dabbled into or involved with).
8. I also renounce and confess as sin any oath which I made to

any false god, and any idolatry in which I have' been involved.

9. Satan, I rebuke you in the name of Jesus, and I close any door which I or my ancestors opened to you and your demons, in the name of Jesus.

10. I renounce satan and all his demons; I declare them my enemies and I command them to get out of my life completely, in the name of Jesus.

11. In the name of Jesus Christ, I now claim deliverance from evil spirits in me. (Joel 2:28). Once and for all, I close the door in my life, to all occult practices and command all spirits related to them to leave me, in Jesus' name.

12. In the name of Jesus, I break any curse of rejection from the womb or illegitimacy in my family, even back to 10 generations, on both sides of my family line. (Deut. 26:2).

13. In the name of Jesus, I now renounce, break and loose myself from all demonic subjection, and any ungodly soul-tie to my mother, father, grandparents or any other person, living or dead, who had ever dominated or controlled me in any way contrary to the will of God and God's word.

14. Lord, I repent and ask You to forgive me if I have ever dominated or controlled anybody in the wrong way.

15. In the name of Jesus Christ, 1 now renounce, break and loose myself and all my descendants from all psychic heredity, demonic holds, psychic powers, bondage, bonds of physical or mental illness, or curses upon my family line as a result of sins, transgressions, iniquities, occult or psychic practices by me, my parents, or any of my ancestors, my spouse, all ex-spouses or their parents, or any of their

ancestors.

16. In the name of Jesus Christ, 1 now renounce, break and loose myself and all my descendants from all evil curses, charms, vexes, spells, jinxes, psychic powers, bewitchment, witchcraft or sorcery, which may have been put upon us by any person or persons; or from any occult or psychic source. I renounce all connected and related spirits and command them to leave me now..

17. I thank you Lord Jesus for setting me free.

18. In the name of Jesus Christ, I command satan and all his demons to loose their hold upon my mind completely.

19. I ask you Father to send Your angels to break all fetters, bands, chains and bonds of whatever sort that the enemy has managed to place on my mind by word or deed.

20. Father, release to me and my family the spirits of: wisdom, counsel, might, knowledge, fear of the Lord, power, love, sound mind, grace and peace.

21. Father, I break and renounce all evil soul-ties with the freemasonry, religious systems, adulterers, drunkards, drug addicts, close friends, cults, etc.

22. Father, I ask you, in the name of Jesus Christ, to send Your angels to gather up the fragments of my soul and restore them to their rightful place in me; and break all earthen storage vessels, including all bonds or bands which have been put upon my soul by any means.

Day 3

1. I claim the restoration of my soul.
2. Let all the pieces of my fragmented mind, will and emotions be brought back into proper and original positions, in Jesus' name.
3. In the name of Jesus Christ, I break all curses issued upon me by witchcraft and, command that they and the spirits from them should return to the senders. (Psalm 109: I7-1- 8).
4. According to Leviticus 26, I now confess the sins of my ancestors: idolatry, witchcraft, occultism, lust, adultery, divorce, perversion, pride, unbelief, rebellion and stubbornness.
5. I claim forgiveness because of the provision in 1 John 1:9. O Lord, I declare the curses broken and lift them from me and my descendants.
6. I command all connected and related spirits to leave me and my family and go wherever Jesus wants them to go.
7. I confess that my body is the temple of the Holy Spirit: redeemed, cleansed and sanctified by the blood of Jesus Christ. Therefore, Satan has no more place in me and no more power over me.

8. Satan, in the name of Jesus Christ, the Son of God, I put you and all your legion on notice that I am attacking you from my position in Christ at the right hand of the Father in the third heaven. I am high above you, your principalities, powers, thrones, dominions, world rulers, rulers of darkness, kings, princes and every angel under your command.

9. Confess Romans 8:15: "For 1 did not receive a spirit that makes one a slave again to fear (bondage); but I received the spirit of sonship (adoption). And by him 1 cry, Abba, Father."

10. Call the spirit you do not desire in your life by name, then issue a command firmly and repeatedly that it should come out, in the name of Lord Jesus.

11. Pray as follows: You spirit of addiction to, or craving for: (pick one by one from the underlisted),
    - acid - caffeine- LSD - peyote
    - alcohol - diet pills - marijuana -
    - amphetamines – downers
    - methadone - STP
    hashish - methedrine TM – sugar -
    aspirin - heroin -mood elevators -
    tranquilizers - barbiturtes - junk food - nicotine,
    in the belly, in the blood, in the lungs, in the mind, in the throat, be paralysed and come out by fire, in the name of Jesus.

12. Pray as follows: You spirit of (pick one by one from the underlisted), come out of my brain and mind, in the name

of Jesus.
- binge - greediness   - nervousness
- bulimia- moodiness   - resentment
compulsiveness - self-reward -
restlessness
frustration - sweet tooth - self-pity.
13. I loose myself from you, in the name of Jesus.
14. I command you to leave me right now, in the mighty
    name of our Lord Jesus Christ.

DESTINY MARCHING ORDERS

YOU MUST MOVE FROM SEEING GOD NOWHERE TO SEEING GOD EVERYWHERE

Your must go from seeing God nowhere to seeing God everywhere. Destiny fulfilment is not a toy to play with. It takes a great deal of efforts to fulfil destinies. When you are journeying to the land of destiny, a lot of water will naturally pass under the bridge. Here is where many people give up as they are unable to see God in their travails. When it appears as if God was nowhere that is when you must know that God is everywhere around you.

A smart lawyer once concluded that God is nowhere. He went as far as placing an inscription in his office entitled, **"GOD IS NOWHERE"**. He had concluded that he was the sole captain of his fate and the architect of his fortune or misfortune. Therefore, he lived his life as if God was nowhere. He was soon proved wrong by his four-year old son.

One day, the boy was brought into his daddy's office. Since daddy was too busy to notice him, he decided to occupy himself with his pencil. He looked up and saw the inscription, **"GOD IS NOWHERE"**. He decided to copy what he had seen. While copying in his faltering handwriting, he wrote the sentence, **"GOD IS NOW HERE."**

The fact that the little boy has been busy writing caught the attention of his busy dad. He stretched his neck to see what the boy had scribbled: GOD IS NOW HERE! He mussed aloud and learnt a great lesson. It took his innocent little boy to tell him that God was very much around him.

Your experience may tell you that God is nowhere but the truth is that God is right here with you. All you need to do is invoke the divine presence through prayers and there would be a floodgate of assurances. His presence will transform the ugly side of your experiences into a new platform for an encounter with the Almighty. You must seek God even if you cannot easily find Him. God will surely reward every diligent seeker.

But without faith it is impossible to please him:
for he that cometh to God must believe that he

is, and that he is a rewarder of them that diligently seek him. Heb 11:6.

When you seek God, you will find your destiny. "God is nowhere," will become God is now here.

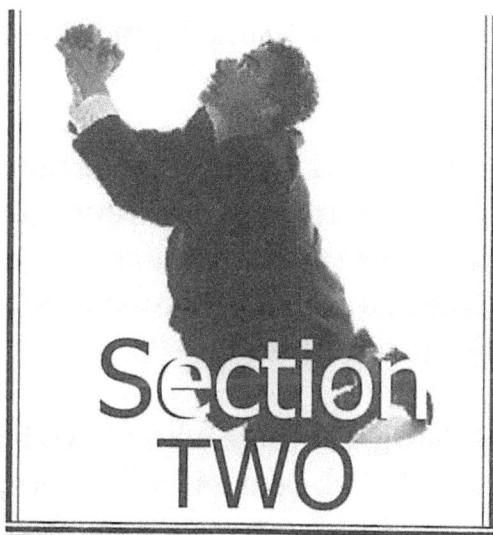

Section TWO

DESTINY CONFESSIONS

I walk not by sight. I walk by faith. My eyes have been anointed with eye salves and I see the invisible, believe the invisible and achieve the impossible.

The Lord has lifted me up and I am seated with Him in heavenly places in Christ Jesus, far above principalities, powers and dominion. And the Lord has put all things under my feet. I use my feet to bruise and destroy all my enemies, even Satan, in Jesus' name. Amen.

I am full of faith in God, I do not doubt, I do not operate in unbelief. I believe and trust God as my Helper, I do not fear anything, for God has not given me the spirit of fear. I have the spirit of power and I have a sound mind through Christ, in Jesus' name. Amen.

My mind is stayed on Christ Jesus; I control my thoughts from thinking evil. In Jesus' name I cast down every imagination and every high thing that exalts itself against the word of God in my life and I command my thoughts and mind to be in obedience to Christ, in Jesus name. Amen.

I am led by the Spirit, for those who are led by the Spirit of God are the sons of God. Because I acknowledge God as my Father, He will order my footsteps and will direct my paths, in Jesus' name. Amen.

The voice of a stranger I will not hear; the leading of a stranger I will not follow. The Lord is my Shepherd. It is He I will hear, it is He I will follow forever, in Jesus' name. Amen.

Today, right now, as I conclude this confession, I cancel all negative confessions I have ever made at anytime in my life, in Jesus' name. I agree with the will of God for my life. I come against all negative confessions spoken by me or by anyone against me. I send the power in the word of God to change every negative confession to positive, in Jesus' name. Amen

Section
THREE

DESTINY SCRIPTURES

My God, my God, why hast thou forsaken me? why art thou so far from helping me, and from the words of my roaring? O my God, I cry in the daytime, but thou hearest not; and in the night season, and am not silent. But thou art holy, O thou that inhabitest the praises of Israel. Our fathers trusted in thee: they trusted, and thou didst deliver them. They cried unto thee, and were delivered: they trusted in thee, and were not confounded. But I am a worm, and no man; a reproach of men, and despised of the people. All they that see me laugh me to scorn: they shoot out the lip, they shake the head saying, He trusted on the LORD that he would deliver him: let him deliver him, seeing he delighted in him. But thou art he that took me out of the womb: thou didst make me hope when I was upon my mother's breasts. I was cast upon thee from the womb: thou art my God from my mother's belly. Be not far from me; for trouble is near; for there is none to help. Many bulls have compassed me: strong bulls of Bashan have beset me round. They gaped upon me with their mouths, as a ravening and a roaring lion. I am poured out like water, and all my bones are out of joint: my heart is like wax; it is melted in the midst of my bowels. My strength is dried up like a potsherd; and my tongue cleaveth to my jaws; and thou hast brought me into the dust of death. For dogs have compassed me: the assembly of the wicked have inclosed me: they pierced my hands and my feet. I may tell all my bones: they look and stare upon me. They part my garments among them, and cast lots upon my vesture. be not thou far from me, O LORD: O my strength, haste thee to help me. Deliver my soul from the sword; my darling from the power of the dog. Save me from the lion's mouth: for thou hast heard me from the horns of the unicorns. I will declare thy name unto my brethren: in the midst of the congregation will I praise thee Psalm 22:1-22.

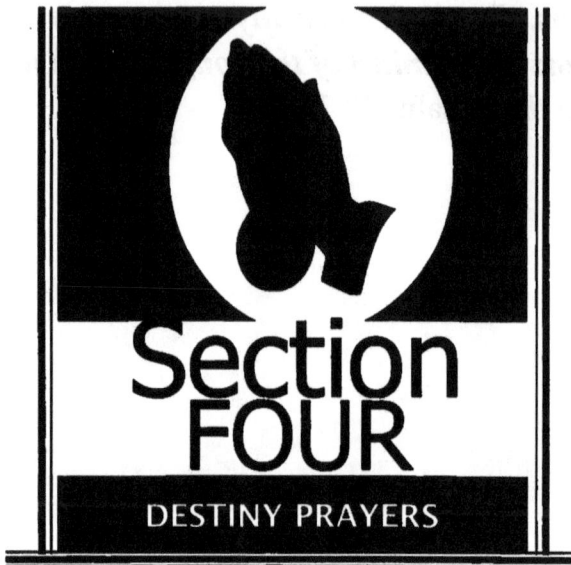

Section FOUR

DESTINY PRAYERS

Day 1

1. Thank God for the purifying power of the fire of the Holy Ghost.
2. I cover myself with the blood of the Lord Jesus.
3. Father, let Your fire that burns away every deposit of the enemy fall upon me, in the name of Jesus.
4. Holy Ghost fire, incubate me, in the name of the Lord Jesus Christ.
5. I reject any evil stamp or seal placed upon me by ancestral spirits, in the name of Jesus.
6. I release myself from every negative anointing, in the name of Jesus

7. Let every door of spiritual leakage be closed, in the name of Jesus.

8. I challenge every organ of my body with the fire of the Holy Spirit (_Lay your right hand methodically on various parts of the body beginning from the head_), in the name of Jesus.

9. Let every human spirit attacking my spirit release me, in the name of Jesus.

10. I reject every spirit of the tail, in the name of Jesus.

11. Sing the song: "Holy Ghost fire, fire fall on me."

12. Let all evil marks on my body be burnt off by the fire of the Holy Spirit, in the name of Jesus.

13. Let the anointing of the Holy Ghost fall upon me and break every negative yoke, in the name of Jesus.

14. Let every garment of hindrance and dirtiness be dissolved by the fire of the Holy Ghost, in the name of Jesus.

15. I command all my chained blessings to be unchained, in the name of Jesus.

16. Let all spiritual cages inhibiting my progress be roasted by the fire of the Holy Spirit, in Jesus' name.

Day 2

1. God of peace, sanctify me wholly, in the name of Jesus.
2. Father Lord, let my body, soul and spirit be preserved blameless unto the coming of our Lord Jesus Christ, in the name of Jesus.
3. Let me be filled with the knowledge of His will, in Jesus' name.
4. Let me be filled with all wisdom and spiritual understanding, in the name of Jesus.
5. Father Lord, help me to walk worthy of and pleasing to the Lord, in the name of Jesus.
6. Father Lord, make me fruitful in every good work, in Jesus' name.
7. Lord, increase me in the knowledge of God.
8. Lord, strengthen me mightily.
9. Father Lord, let me be filled with the spirit of wisdom and understanding in the knowledge of Christ, in the name of Jesus.
10. Father Lord, let the eyes of my understanding be enlightened, in the name of Jesus.
11. Father Lord, let me be strengthened with might by Your Spirit in the inner man, in the name of Jesus.
12. Father Lord, let Christ dwell in my heart by faith, in Jesus' name.
13. Father Lord, let me be rooted and grounded in love, in Jesus' name.

14. Lord, let me be filled with all fullness of God.
15. God, help me comprehend the breadth, length, depth and height of the love of Christ, in the name of Jesus
16. Let the word of the Lord have free course and be glorified in me, in the name of Jesus.
17. Let the Lord of peace give me peace in all areas of my life, in the name of Jesus.
18. Let utterance be given unto me to make known the mystery of the gospel, in the name of Jesus.
19. Lord, perfect what is lacking in my faith.
20. Lord, perfect Your good work in me.
21. Lord, make me perfect unto Your good work.
22. Lord, enrich me in all utterances and knowledge.
23. Let the grace of the Lord Jesus Christ be with me, in Jesus' name.
24. Father Lord, inject into me your spiritual vitamins that will make me spiritually healthy, in the name of Jesus.
25. Father Lord, inject into me spiritual vitamins that will boost my appetite to eat Your word, in the name of Jesus.
26. Father Lord, infuse into my blood spiritual vitamins that will produce hunger and thirst for prayers, in the name of Jesus.
27. Let God inject into me spiritual vitamins that will clear my vision and strengthen its clarity, in the name of Jesus.
28. Lord God, inject into me spiritual vitamins that will sustain me in evil days.
29. Lord God, inject into me divine immunity that will always kill spiritual germs and evil deposits in me.

30. Lord God, inject into me the spiritual energy that will make me walk tirelessly with you.
31. Lord God, feed me with the food of the champions.
32. Lord God, boost my energy to run the race set before me.
33. I receive the comforting anointing and power in the Holy Ghost, in the name of Jesus.
34. I receive the unsearchable wisdom in the Holy Ghost, in the name of Jesus.
35. I take the shield of faith to quench every fiery dart of the enemy, in the name of Jesus.
36. I run into the name of the Lord which is a strong tower and I am safe.
37. Father Lord, always make me drink from Your everlasting well of joy, in the name of Jesus.
38. Thank God for the new spiritual height He has lifted you to.

Day 3

1. Thank God for the revelation power of the Holy Spirit.
2. Lord, give unto me the spirit of revelation and wisdom in the knowledge of Yourself.
3. Lord, make Your way plain before my face on this issue.
4. Lord, remove spiritual cataract from my eyes.
5. Lord, forgive me for every false motive or thought that has ever been formed in my heart since the day I was born.
6. Lord, forgive me for any lie that I have ever told against any person, system or organisation.
7. Lord, deliver me from the bondage and sin of spiritual laziness.
8. Lord, open my eyes to see all I should on this issue.
9. Lord, teach me deep and secret things.
10. Lord, reveal to me every secret behind any problem that I have.
11. Lord, bring to light every thing planned against me in darkness.

DESTINY MARCHING ORDERS

YOU MUST GO FROM BEING ORDINARY TO EXTRAORDINARY

You must go from being ordinary to becoming an extraordinary person. There are two strands of life: the ordinary and the extraordinary. Most people have chosen the part that is ordinary. Only very few dare take the bull by the horn and go first class by becoming extraordinary.

There is a tiny gap between the ordinary and the extraordinary life. To move from the ordinary and become extraordinary, you only need to go further when others have concluded that moving ahead is tasking. Most people have lost the extra shine of their destiny by giving up at the edge of their breakthroughs. The ordinary class is overcrowded with people who are jostling for non-existent space. But the extraordinary class is so roomy when the issue of destiny is concerned.

If your destiny is ordinary, you may struggle from dawn to dusk without coming up with any tangible achievement. But if you are ready to make spirited efforts and become exceptional in your chosen field or career, the whole world will seek your attention.

Ordinary people are generally far from being celebrated. Extraordinary people easily get to a point where they become celebrated. The truth is that ordinary people are tolerated while extraordinary people are celebrated.

There are prices to be paid for becoming extraordinary. These include:

1. Fervent and uncommon prayers.
2. Hard work.
3. A knack for exceeding limits.
4. Unusual sacrifices.
5. Spartan discipline.
6. Addiction to excellence.
7. Persistence.
8. Faithfulness.
9. Paying careful attention to details.
10. Consistency.

You must accumulate the ingredients of an extraordinary destiny. You must pray until the extraordinary factors in your destiny are brought to the fore. By the time you make maximum use of your potentials, the whole world will notice the extraordinary qualities that made your destiny stand out.

Paul the Apostle reminds us of what it is to be an extraordinary character:

> *For I am the least of the apostles, that am not meet to be called an apostle, because I persecuted the church of God. But by the grace of God I am what I am: and his grace which was bestowed upon me was not in vain; but I laboured more abundantly than they all: yet not I, but the grace of God which was with me.* 1 Cor 15:9-10.

Section TWO

DESTINY CONFESSIONS

I am not ordinary. I am extra-ordinary. I am not only the best, I am created to be the best. I shall be above only. I shall not be beneath. I have said goodbye to mediocrity. I have moved up from the ordinary or the average class. God has endowed me with excellent qualities. Now is the season of the manifestation of the sons of God. From today the world will begin to behold the glory of God upon my life. I shall emerge victorious. The extra-ordinary qualities of God will be seen in my destiny.

My body is the temple of the Holy Spirit. The Spirit of God dwells inside me, in Jesus' name. Amen.

I am a container for the fire of the Holy Ghost and the power of God resides inside me, in Jesus' name. Amen.

As I speak the word of God, I send it to go forth as fuel of unquenchable fire to consume all my enemies, in the name of Jesus. Amen.

I receive it to encircle me and protect me from all my enemies, in Jesus' name. Amen.

I am fire-proof to all the enemies fire and weapons of war against me, in Jesus' name. Amen.

I am a danger to the whole kingdom of darkness. I am as a live wire. Anyone that touches or tries to touch me shall be electrocuted and set ablaze forever, in Jesus' name. Amen.

The word of God says, "Never touch or try to harm a child of God". I am the apple of God's eyes. Anyone that intends or plots evil against me, God shall destroy, in Jesus' name. Amen.

I believe and I receive the blood of Jesus Christ, that was shed for me on the cross of Calvary. I am redeemed by the blood of Jesus. Right now, I take the blood of Jesus Christ and I use it to set a boundary round about me, in Jesus' name. Amen.

I receive the blood of Jesus Christ upon me and upon the house where I live, in Jesus' name. Amen.

The angels have been ordered by God to take charge of me in all my ways, and I receive them, in Jesus' name. They go ahead of me wherever I go and in whatever I do. They go forth and make all my crooked ways straight, in Jesus' name. Amen.

Section
THREE

DESTINY SCRIPTURES

Oh that thou wouldest rend the heavens, that thou wouldest come down, that the mountains might flow down at thy presence, As when the melting fire burneth, the fire causeth the waters to boil, to make thy name known to thine adversaries, that the nations may tremble at thy presence! When thou didst terrible things which we looked not for, thou camest down, the mountains flowed down at thy presence. For since the beginning of the world men have not heard, nor perceived by the ear, neither hath the eye seen, O God, beside thee, what he hath prepared for him that waiteth for him. Isa 64:1-4.

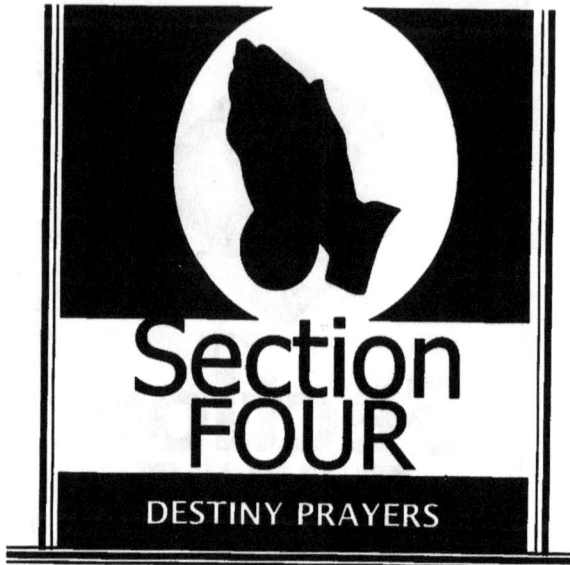

Section FOUR

DESTINY PRAYERS

Day 1

1. I release myself from every ancestral demonic pollution, in the name of Jesus.
2. I release myself from every demonic pollution emanating from my parent's religion, in the name of Jesus.
3. I release myself from demonic pollution emanating from my past involvement in any demonic religion, in the name of Jesus.
4. I break and loose myself from every idol related association, in the name of Jesus.
5. I release myself from every dream pollution, in Jesus' name.
6. Let every satanic attack against my life in my dreams be converted to victory, in the name of Jesus.

7. Let all rivers, trees, forests, evil companions, evil pursuers, pictures of dead relatives, snakes, spirit husbands, spirit wives and masquerades manipulated against me in the dream, be completely destroyed by the power in the blood of the Lord Jesus.

8. I command every evil plantation in my life: **Come out with all your roots, in the name of Jesus!** (*Lay your hands on your stomach and keep repeating the emphasised area.*)

9. Evil strangers in my body, come out of your hiding places, in the name of Jesus.

10. I disconnect any conscious or unconscious link with demonic caterers, in the name of Jesus.

11. Let all avenues of eating or drinking spiritual poisons be closed, in the name of Jesus.

12. I cough out and vomit any food eaten from the table of the devil, in the name of Jesus. (*Cough them out and vomit them in faith. Prime the expulsion.*)

13. Let all negative materials circulating in my blood stream be evacuated, in the name of Jesus.

14. I drink the blood of Jesus. (*Physically swallow and drink it in faith, keep doing this for some time.*)

15. (*Lay one hand on your head and the other on your stomach or navel and begin to pray like this*): Holy Ghost fire, burn from the top of my head to the soles of my feet. Mention every organ of your body: your kidney, liver, intestine, blood, etc. You must not rush at this level, because the fire will actually come and you may start feeling the heat.

16. I cut myself off from every spirit of... (mention the name

of your place of birth), in the name of Jesus.

17. I cut myself off from every territorial spirit and curse, in Jesus' name,

18. Holy Ghost fire, purge my life.

19. .I claim my complete deliverance, in the name of Jesus, from the spirit of... (mention those things you do not desire in your life).

20. I break the hold of any evil power over my life, in Jesus' name

21. Jesus, I thank You for the purging and for the in-filling of Your revival fire.

Day 2

1. Holy Spirit, multiply your grace upon my life, in the name of Jesus.
2. Anointing of wisdom, fall upon my inner man, in the name of Jesus.
3. Holy Ghost fire, open the eyes of my spirit, in the name of Jesus.
4. Oh Lord, let all the angels assigned to assist me in my ministry receive fire, in the name of Jesus.
5. Any power that has arrested my angels, be arrested and let my angels be released, in the name of Jesus.
6. Mighty hand of God, fall upon me for my ministry and protection, in the name of Jesus.
7. Oh Lord, let me and my descendants dwell under the shadow of the Almighty all the days of our lives, in Jesus' name.
8. Oh Lord, keep me, my ministry, my family and my descendants after me in Your pavilion, in the name of Jesus; for in your pavilion, evil arrows cannot locate me.
9. Evil arrows that came into my life by night, jump up and come out of my life by night, in the name of Jesus.
10. Oh Lord God of Elijah, arise in Your power and let all my enemies fall before me, in the name of Jesus.
11. Oh Lord, whenever my enemies plan any attack against me in the future, let their counsel fall into foolishness, in the name of Jesus.

12. Oh Lord, whenever my enemies take evil decisions against me, let your truth deliver me according to Thy Word in the name of Jesus. (Pray also for those who are victims of accusations and slander from brethren in the house of God).

13. Lord, Man of War, destroy the teeth of all those the devil will use against me in Your sanctuary, in the name of Jesus.

14. Lord, break me and mould me for your glory, in the name of Jesus.

15. Every synagogue of Satan erected against me, fall down before me now for I am the beloved of the Lord, in the name of Jesus.

16. Anything in me that will allow the arrow of the enemy to prosper, be removed now, in the name of Jesus.

17. Every demonic alteration of my destiny, loose your hold upon my life and come out of my foundation, in the name of Jesus.

18. All powers behind demonic alteration of my destiny, die, in the name of Jesus.

Day 3

1. Any power behind demonic alteration of my destiny and virtues, die, in the name of Jesus.
2. Demonic marriage, loose your hold over my life and be purged out of my foundation, in the name of Jesus.
3. Every strange child assigned to me in the dream, be roasted by fire, in the name of Jesus.
4. I command the fire of God to pursue all strange women and children assigned to me in the dream, in the' name of Jesus.
5. Every evil laying on of hands, loose your hold over my life and be purged out of my foundation, in the name of Jesus.
6. Evil idols from my father's house, fight against idols in my mother's house and destroy yourselves, in Jesus' name.
7. Every idol in the city of my birth holding down my destiny, be roasted by fire, in the name of Jesus.
8. Every demonic authority attacking my life as a result of my past sexual partners, be roasted by fire, in the name of Jesus.
9. Every demon activated against me, go back to your owner, in the name of Jesus.
10. All demons and principalities assigned against me, be decommissioned, in the name of Jesus.

11. Every evil voice rising up against my glory, be silenced, in the name of Jesus.

12. Holy Spirit of God, do something new in my life today, in the name of Jesus.

13. Oh Lord, make me an instrument of revival in Your hand.

14. I shake off powers of demotion in my life, in the name of Jesus.

15. Thou serpent of demotion, release my glory, in the name of Jesus.

16. Oh heaven, arise and release me from captivity, in the name of Jesus.

DESTINY MARCHING ORDERS

YOU MUST MOVE FROM BEING DEFECTIVE TO BEING EFFECTIVE

You must go from being defective to being effective. The field of destiny is littered with carcasses and bones of men and women who were defective in one way or the other. One of the problems of life is that the moment people are defective, the society has no place for them. But God looks at this issue differently. The Bible likens Him to a potter.

When the potter discovers that a particular clay has been disfigured, he will not give up. The patience of the potter here represents the patience and the persistence of the Almighty.

The word which came to Jeremiah from the LORD, saying, Arise, and go down to the potter's house, and there I will cause thee to hear my words. Then I went down to the potter's house, and, behold, he wrought a work on the wheels. And the vessel that he made of clay was marred in the hand of the potter: so he made it again another vessel, as seemed good to the potter to make it. Then the word of the LORD came to me, saying, O house of Israel, cannot I do with you as this potter? saith the LORD. Behold, as the clay is in the potter's hand, so are ye in mine hand, O house of Israel. At what instant I shall speak concerning a nation, and concerning a kingdom, to pluck up, and to pull down, and to destroy it; If that nation, against whom I have pronounced, turn from their evil, I will repent of the evil that I thought to do unto them. Jer. 18:1-8.

It is quite easy to abandon a marred vessel, but God keeps giving us new chances so that our destinies can be formed into what He intends it to be. If something is defective in your destiny, you should not give up on yourself. You must move from being defective to being effective.

You must be able to know where things have gone wrong. You may need to carry out a personal analysis of yourself. Take an inventory and make a list of all your weaknesses. Do not sweep anything under the carpet. Do not pamper yourself. Get rid of the defective factors that are militating against your destiny. You must allow God to repair, restore and fashion you according to His divine foresight, plan and purpose. These cannot take place without a great deal of aggressive prayers.

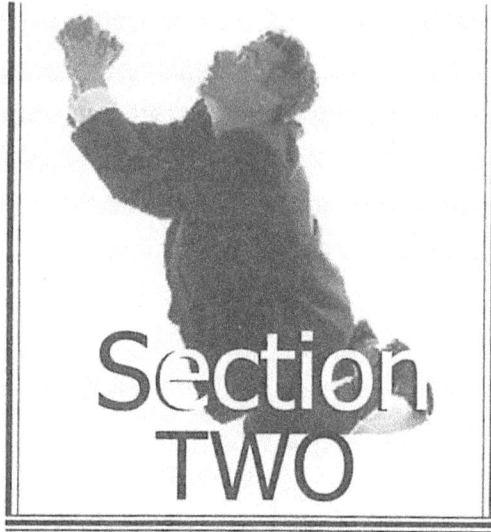

Section TWO

DESTINY CONFESSIONS

I am fearfully and wonderfully made. I am a product of divinity. There is no defeat in the product of the Almighty. I am a specimen of perfection, a symbol of excellence and an example of the best God can do. God has taken me from being defective to being effective. My God will perfect that which concerns me. He has removed all blemishes in my label and converted my minus to plus. God has visited me and cancelled all negative handwriting on my destiny. Labels associated with defects are gone. God has transferred me to an emblem of optimum productivity and effectiveness.

Therefore, there is now no condemnation for those who are in Christ Jesus; who walk not after the dictates of the flesh but after the dictates of the spirit. For the law of our new being, which is the law of the spirit of life in Christ, has freed me from the law of sin and death. I am separated by God through the redeeming power in the blood of Christ my Messiah, the Author and Finisher of my faith, from every tie with ancestral covenants, curses and guardian spirits.

I know who I am in Christ. I have been purchased by the blood of Jesus Christ that was shed for me on the Cross of Calvary. I am a child of God. I am called by the name of the Lord. I was bought by the blood of the Lamb of God. I believe in the power of the blood of Jesus. Jesus has translated my life from the kingdom of darkness into His own marvellous kingdom of light and peace. I now belong to the kingdom of God. I have the keys of the kingdom of God in my hands to bind and loose. I have the authority to trample under my feet, serpents, scorpions and all the powers of the enemy.

Through death, Jesus Christ has destroyed Satan, who had the power of death and hell. Jesus has delivered my life from death and domination. Before Jesus ascended, He first of all descended into the lower parts of the earth and stripped the devil of all his powers over me. Jesus has taken from Satan the keys of death and hell and has given me the keys of life. By virtue of the work Jesus Christ did on the cross, I have power over all the powers of the enemy. He has wiped out all the handwriting of requirements that were against me, took them out of the way and nailed them to His own cross. He disarmed principalities and powers and made a show of them openly, triumphing over them in it.

It is written that God will light my lamp and enlighten my darkness. But every satanic agent or power, oppressing me, shall grope in the daytime as in thick darkness. Therefore, I ask that as I make these confessions, the Lord will be my strength to run through a troop, to leap over any wall, to pursue and overtake my enemies, to recover my stolen properties, to beat them small as the dust, to withstand and overcome all spiritual oppositions and distractions.

Section
THREE

DESTINY SCRIPTURES

Look down from heaven, and behold from the habitation of thy holiness and of thy glory: where is thy zeal and thy strength, the sounding of thy bowels and of thy mercies toward me? are they restrained? Doubtless thou art our father, though Abraham be ignorant of us, and Israel acknowledge us not: thou, O LORD, art our father, our redeemer; thy name is from everlasting. O LORD, why hast thou made us to err from thy ways, and hardened our heart from thy fear? Return for thy servants' sake, the tribes of thine inheritance. The people of thy holiness have possessed it but a little while: our adversaries have trodden down thy sanctuary. We are thine: thou never barest rule over them; they were not called by thy name. Isa 63:15-19.

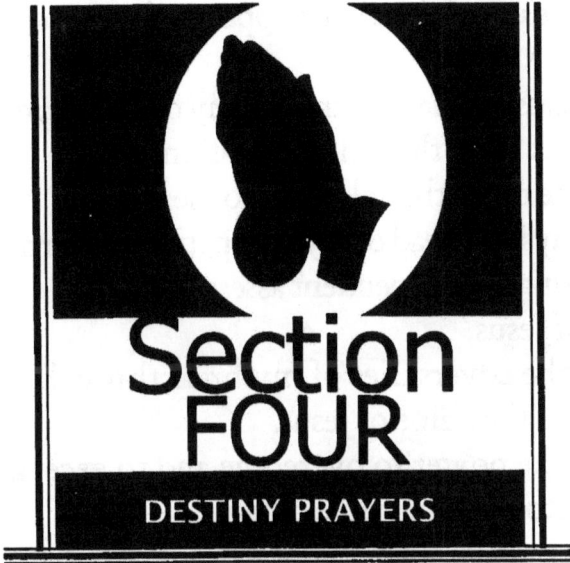

Section FOUR
DESTINY PRAYERS

Day 1

1. Let all evil competitors stumble and fall, in the name of Jesus.
2. Let all my adversaries make mistakes that will advance my cause, in the name of Jesus.
3. I send confusion into the camp of all evil counsellors planning against my progress, in the name of Jesus.
4. I command darkness into the camp of the enemy, in Jesus' name.
5. I remove my name from the book of failure and demonic side-track, in the name of Jesus.
6. Lord, give me the power to:

a.   Make use of the divine opportunity presented to me.

b.   Possess more wisdom than my competitors.

c.   Drink from the well of salvation.

d.   Make my paths unknown to the enemy

e.   always be ahead of my competitors in terms of favour and independent assessment, in   t h e name of Jesus.

7.   Let all the adversaries of my breakthroughs be put to shame, in the name of Jesus.

8.   I claim the power to overcome and to excel among all competitors, in the name of Jesus.

9.   I command all human woes to find me untouchable, in Jesus' name.

10. Let any decision by any panel be favourable unto me, in the name of Jesus,

11. I remove my name from the book of failure and retrogression, in the name of Jesus.

12. Let the anointing of the overcomer fall upon my life, in the name of Jesus,

13. I receive wisdom, knowledge and understanding to subdue all competitors, in the name of Jesus.

14. Let every negative word and pronouncement against my success be completely nullified, in the name of Jesus.

15. All competitors with me in this issue will find my defeat impossible, in the name of Jesus,

16. Father Lord, let your wisdom and power be upon me in a measure that cannot be quantified, in the name of Jesus.

17. I claim supernatural wisdom to answer all questions in a way that will advance my cause, in the name of Jesus.
18. I receive the anointing for supernatural breakthrough in this matter, in the name of Jesus.
19. Thank the Lord for the answers.

Day 2

1. I break every hold of witchcraft working against my life, in the name of Jesus.
2. I command a change in all unprofitable situations in my life, in the name of Jesus.
3. I command my battle to change to blessings, in Jesus' name.
4. Let every mountain of satanic confrontation be disgraced, in the name of Jesus.
5. Let every mountain of impossibility be dashed to pieces, in the name of Jesus.
6. Let new wells spring up in my desert, in the name of Jesus.
7. Lord, bear me up on eagle's wings before my enemies.
8. Lord, anoint my eyes to see my divine opportunities.
9. I refuse to allow my past to influence my future negatively.
10. Let every satanic battle confronting me, fall apart, in Jesus' name.
11. I bind the strongman of financial embarrassment, in Jesus' name.
12. I declare myself free from the plagues of spiritual Egypt, in the name Jesus.
13. I command all crooked and difficult areas of my life to begin to yield testimonies, in the name Jesus.
14. Let the spirit of excellence manifest in every area of my life, in the name Jesus.
15. Let the fear of me fill the mind of the enemy and let them panic, in the name Jesus.

16. My year shall not be in struggle but in prosperity, in Jesus' name.
17. Let the oppressors drown in their own Red Sea, in Jesus' name.
18. I receive power to leap over every wall that the enemy has built, in the name of Jesus.
19. Let the enemy fall into his own trap, in the name of Jesus
20. Lord, make my miracle invisible to my enemies.
21. Lord, re-organise my system to confuse evil observers.
22. I resist all spiritual sabotage and cunning attacks, in the name Jesus.
23. Let the fire of God protect my miracle, in the name Jesus.
24. Let the root of every night terror dry up, in the name Jesus.
25. Let all the weapons of the enemy work against them, in the name Jesus.
26. The mockery of my enemies shall result in my advancement, in the name Jesus.
27. Lord, turn my mourning to dancing and my tears to joy.
28. Let the sword and shield of the enemy turn against him, in the name Jesus.
29. Let attack by household wickedness melt away, in Jesus' name.
30. Every Goliath defying by prayers, be impotent, in Jesus' name.
31. Lord, display Your power against every unrepentant opposition in my life.
32. Let evil intention of mockers turn against them, in Jesus' name.

33. Lord, convert my opposition to promotion.
34. I uproot every evil testimony, in the name of Jesus.
35. I thank You, O Lord, for the deliverance.

Day 3

1.   Let all my enemies fall into their own traps, in the name of Jesus.
2.   Lord, convert my struggle to prosperity.
3.   Lord, I refuse to let You go unless You bless me.
4.   Every evil preparation against my life, be frustrated, in Jesus' name.
5.   Lord, let my joy, peace and blessings be multiplied.
6.   Blood of Jesus, disconnect my life from failure at the edge of breakthroughs, in the name of Jesus.
7.   I refuse to reap any evil harvest in every department of my life, in the name of Jesus.
8.   Let divine favour in every blessing of life be my lot, in Jesus' name.
9.   I cut off and reject every inherited poverty, in the name of Jesus.
10.   Let the foundation of my life be repaired to carry divine prosperity, in the name of Jesus.
11.   Let every territorial power hindering answers to my prayers be brought down to the pit, in the name of Jesus.
12.   I refuse to offer unacceptable offerings, in the name of Jesus.
13.   I refuse to run ahead of God in all my endeavours, in Jesus' name.

14. I refuse to ask in contrast to God's will, in the name of Jesus.

15. I refuse to harbour any prayer killer in any department of my life, in the name of Jesus.

DESTINY MARCHING ORDERS

YOU MUST MOVE FROM BEING LUKEWARM TO BEING ON FIRE

You must go from being lukewarm to being on fire. For your destiny to be fulfilled you need an appreciable dose of fire. There are too many forces militating against destiny in this environment. If you are lukewarm, you are providing a fertile ground for evil spirits to prey on your destiny. Those who are lukewarm are neither here nor there. They are not cold and they are not hot. If there is any category of people who easily fall victim of satanic predators, it is the class of people who are lukewarm. God has declared that he would spew out those who are lukewarm.

But I have a few things against thee, because thou hast there them that hold the doctrine of Balaam, who taught Balac to cast a stumblingblock before the children of Israel, to eat things sacrificed unto idols, and to commit fornication. So hast thou also them that hold the doctrine of the Nicolaitans, which thing I hate. Repent; or else I will come unto thee quickly, and will fight against them with the sword of my mouth. He that hath an ear, let him hear what the Spirit saith unto the churches; To him that overcometh will I give to eat of the hidden manna, and will give him a white stone, and in the stone a new name written, which no man knoweth saving he that receiveth it. And unto the angel of the church in Thyatira write; These things saith the Son of God, who hath his eyes like unto a flame of fire, and his feet are like fine brass; I know thy works, and charity, and service, and faith, and thy patience, and thy works; and the last to be more than the first. Rev 2:14-19.

God wants you to be on fire. If you are cold or lukewarm, there is no guarantee that God will protect your destiny. God has made it clear that He prefers that you are on fire. What you need to move your destiny forward is to receive the fire of the

Holy Ghost. Your destiny needs the baptism of fire. There are three types of baptism.

1.   Water baptism.
2.   Baptism of the Holy Ghost.
3.   Baptism of fire.

On the issue of destiny, the baptism of fire is the most important. When the baptism of fire falls upon you, you will not find it difficult to do away with the attire of Jezebel or any material of the enemy. When you become a carrier of fire, you will become too hot for the enemies to handle. If they come against you in one way, they will flee in seven other directions because there is too much fire upon you.

Fire will protect your destiny. It will jumpstart your destiny to greatness. It will mould your destiny. It will make you a sign and a wonder. It will make your destiny too hot for the kingdom of darkness to tamper with.

Section TWO

DESTINY CONFESSIONS

I am a carrier of the fire of the Holy Ghost. I have moved from lukewarmness to the vibrancy and the warmth of the Holy Ghost. There is no place for coldness or lukewarmness in my life. There is fire in my bones. My heart is aglow with the fire of the Holy Ghost. My destiny is enveloped with the burning fire of the Holy Ghost. Lukewarmness is gone. Spiritual coldness has vanished. The power of God has entered my bones. I am on fire. I am set ablaze for victory. My life has moved to the fast lane of spiritual aggression. Every coldness of darkness has been expelled. From now on, my life shall remain a specimen of what the fire of the Holy Ghost can do. My spiritual battery has been fully charged with the current of Holy Ghost fire.

Phil 3:10, 14 says:

> *That I may know him, and the power of his resurrection, and the fellowship of his sufferings, being made conformable unto his death; I press toward the mark for the prize of the high calling of God in Christ Jesus.*

I am commanded and empowered by my God to subdue and to exercise dominion. Though I am made a little lower than the angels, God has crowned me with glory and honour and has also made me to have dominion over all the works of His hands. The devil that was against my authority as God's representative on earth has been destroyed by Christ and the keys of the kingdom of heaven are given to me. And because I am a member of the body of Christ, which is the church, the gate of hell cannot prevail against me.

I am a branch in the vine; Jesus Christ is the true vine. Because I abide in Him, I am full of the fruit of the Spirit. I am full of love, joy, peace, long-suffering, kindness, goodness, faithfulness, gentleness and self-control. Because the grace of God is upon my life as the light of His glory, I am full of divine favour; I am a partaker of all heaven's spiritual blessings. I am an overcomer. The Bible says whosoever is born of God overcomes the world, and this is the victory that overcomes the world, even my faith. In faith I overcome ungodly worry, anxiety, heaviness of spirit, sorrow, depression, lust of the eyes and lust of the flesh. In faith I have overcome all the tricks of the devil, for it is written, greater is Jesus Christ that dwells in me than the devil that is in the world.

No weapon that is formed against me shall prosper. In righteousness I am established; I am far from oppression, for I shall not fear any terror, for it shall not come near me. The Lord shall cover me with His feather. Because I have made Him my dwelling place, evil shall not befall me; I shall tread upon the lion and the cobra, and surely the Lord will always deliver me from the snare of the fowlers. I have spoken with the tongue of the learned, and as it is written, I shall be justified by the words of my mouth. I ask that the word of God, which I have confessed, begins to transform me from what I am now to the original image God has designed me to be.

I ask that the blood of the Lamb of God, Jesus Christ of Nazareth, wipe away from me every mark of reproach, whether physical or spiritual. I ask for the blood of Jesus to erase every evil and negative names I have ever been called. I cease to be a picture of failure. I nullify every negative report ever made about me. I cease to be abased, rejected, forsaken, desolate and downcast. I begin to manifest expressly every good thing God has written about me in His word. I begin to look fearfully and wonderfully made. I begin to operate at the head and not the tail. I begin to be a true worshipper of Jehovah El Shaddai and I begin to continually praise Him and confess positively, in the precious name of our Lord Jesus Christ of Nazareth. Amen.

Section
THREE

DESTINY SCRIPTURES

The people that walked in darkness have seen a great light: they that dwell in the land of the shadow of death, upon them hath the light shined. Thou hast multiplied the nation, and not increased the joy: they joy before thee according to the joy in harvest, and as men rejoice when they divide the spoil. For thou hast broken the yoke of his burden, and the staff of his shoulder, the rod of his oppressor, as in the day of Midian. For every battle of the warrior is with confused noise, and garments rolled in blood; but this shall be with burning and fuel of fire. Isa 9:2-5.

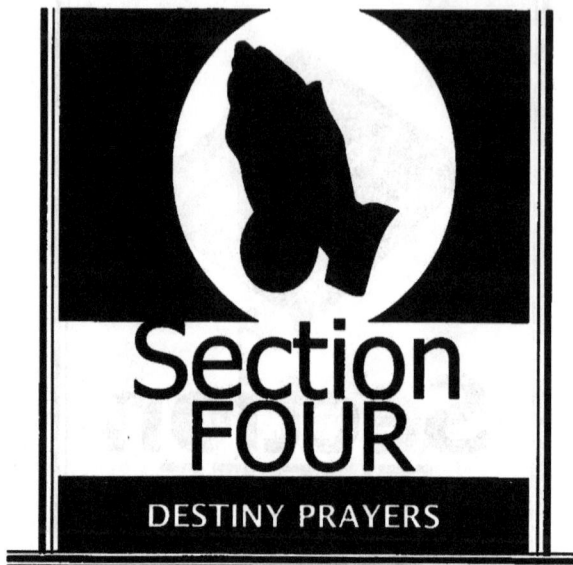

Day 1

1. Lord, cleanse all the soiled part of my life.
2. Lord, refresh every dry area of my life.
3. Lord, heal every wounded part of my life.
4. Lord, bend every evil rigidity in my life.
5. Lord, re-align every satanic straying in my life.
6. Lord, let the fire of the Holy Spirit warm every satanic freeze in my life.
7. Lord, give me a life that kills death.
8. Lord, kindle in me the fire of charity.
9. Lord, glue me together where I am opposed to myself.
10. Lord, enrich me with Your gift.

11. Lord, quicken me and increase my desire for the things of heaven.
12. By your rulership, O Lord, let the lust of the flesh in my life die.
13. Lord Jesus, increase daily in my life.
14. Lord Jesus, maintain your gifts in my life.
15. Lord, refine and purge my heart, in the name of Jesus.
16. Holy Spirit, inflame and fire my heart, in the name of Jesus.
17. Lord Jesus, lay your hands upon me and quench every rebellion in me.
18. Holy Ghost fire, begin to burn away every self-centeredness in me, in the name of Jesus.
19. Father Lord, breathe your life-giving breath into my soul, in the name of Jesus.
20. Lord, make me ready to go wherever you send me
21. Lord Jesus, never let me shut you out.
22. Lord Jesus, never let me try to limit you to my capacity.
23. Lord Jesus, work freely in me and through me.
24. Lord, purify the channels of my life.
25. Let your heat, O Lord, consume my will, in the name of Jesus.
26. Let the flame of the Holy Spirit blaze upon the altar of my heart, in the name of Jesus.
27. Lord Jesus, come like blood into my vein.
28. Lord, order my spirit and fashion my life in Your will.
29. Lord, let Your fire burn in me all that is not holy in your will.
30. Lord, let Your fire generate power in my life.

31. Lord Jesus, impart to me thoughts higher than my own thoughts.
32. Holy Spirit, come as dew and refresh me, in the name of Jesus.
33. Holy Spirit, guide me in the way of liberty, in the name of Jesus.
34. Holy Spirit, blow upon me such that sin would no more find place in me, in the name of Jesus.
35. Holy Spirit, where my love is cold warm me up, in Jesus' name.
36. Thank God for His mighty presence in your life.
37. Let my hand become the sword of fire to cut down evil trees, in the name of Jesus.
38. Let my feet, become the thunder of God. As I stamp them let them deafen the enemy, in the name of Jesus.
39. Let the spiritual rag of poverty in my life be paralysed, in Jesus' name.
40. Let the enemy of excellence in my life be converted to my promotion, in the name of Jesus.
41. Let every past satanic achievement in my life be converted to my promotion, in the name of Jesus.
42. Lord, let the shame of my enemies be multiplied greatly.
43. Lord, let the defeat and disgrace of the enemy of my progress be multiplied beyond measure.
44. Let every power planning to put my life upside down fall down and now, in the name of Jesus.
45. I paralyse every satanic inspiration targeted against me, in the name of Jesus.

46. I barricade my life from every satanic opinion, in the name of Jesus.
47. Let my divinely-appointed helpers begin to locate me from now, in the name of Jesus.
48. Every lame glory, receive life now, in the name of Jesus.
49. Thank God for answers to your prayers.

Day 2

1. All my blessings imprisoned by the grave, come forth, in the name of Jesus.
2. I release my blessings from the hands of all dead relatives, in the name of Jesus.
3. I withdraw my blessings from the hands of all dead enemies, in the name of Jesus
4. I disgrace every witchcraft burial, in the name of Jesus
5. Just as the grave could not detain Jesus, no power will detain my miracles, in the name of Jesus
6. That which hinders me from greatness, give way now, in the name of Jesus.
7. Whatsoever has been done against me with the ground be neutralised, in the name of Jesus.
8. Every unfriendly friend, be exposed, in the name of Jesus
9. Anything representing my image in the spirit world, I withdraw you, in the name of Jesus.
10. All the camps of my enemies, receive confusion, in the name of Jesus.
11. Lord, empower my life with Your authority over every demonic force, in the name of Jesus
12. Lord, let all the impossible begin to become possible for me in every department of my life, in the name of Jesus.
13. Lord, take me from where I am to where You want me to be, in the name of Jesus.

14. Lord, make a way for me where there is no way, in the name of Jesus.
15. Lord, grant me the power to be fulfilled, successful and prosperous in life, in the name of Jesus.
16. Lord, break me up in every department of my life and re-mould me, in the name of Jesus.
17. Lord, let me break through into dumfounding miracles in all areas of my life, in the name of Jesus.
18. Lord, make me to break out of every obstacle on my way to progress in life, in the name of Jesus.
19. Lord, establish me in truth, godliness and faithfulness.
20. Lord, add flavour to my work, in the name of Jesus
21. Lord, add increase to my work, in the name of Jesus.
22. Lord, add profitability to my work, in the name Jesus.
23. Lord, promote and preserve my life, in the name of Jesus
24. I reject the plans and agenda of the enemies against my life, in the name of Jesus.
25. I reject the assignments and weapons of the enemy against my life, in the name of Jesus.
26. Let every weapon and evil design against me fail totally, in the name of Jesus.
27. I reject premature death, in the name of Jesus.
28. I reject nightmares and sudden destruction, in the name of Jesus.
29. I reject dryness in my walk with God, in the name of Jesus.
30. I reject financial debt, in the name of Jesus.

31. I reject lack and famine in my life, in the name of Jesus.
32. I reject physical and spiritual accidents in my going in and coming out, in the name of Jesus.
33. I reject sickness in my spirit, soul and body, in the name of Jesus.
34. I stand against every work of evil in my life, in the name of Jesus.
35. I overcome powerlessness, confusion and every attack of the enemy, in the name of Jesus.
36. I command spiritual divorce between me and every power of darkness, in the name of Jesus.
37. Let every poison and arrow of the enemy be neutralised in my life, in the name of Jesus.
38. I break every yoke of unfruitfulness in my life, in the name of Jesus.
39. I cancel the plans and the mark of the enemy upon my life, in the name of Jesus.
40. Lord Jesus, break all harmful genetic ties in my life, in the name of Jesus.
41. Thank God for answered prayers.

Day 3

1. Thank the Lord for the privilege of your working in His vineyard.
2. Since many are called but few are chosen, thank the Lord for choosing you. .
3. Bring quality repentance to the Lord.
4. I shall not be a misfired arrow in the hands of my Maker, in the name of Jesus.
5. Any foundational power working against my calling, be destroyed, in the name of Jesus.
6. Every yoke working against spiritual growth in my life, be broken, in the name of Jesus.
7. The enemy will not make me a bad example, in the name of Jesus.
8. Every destructive habit designed to waste my calling, die, in the name of Jesus.
9. Power of good finishing, come upon my destiny, in the name of Jesus. .
10. Every area of incomplete deliverance in my life, receive complete deliverance by fire, in the name of Jesus.
11. Every spiritual cataract, clear away from my vision, in the name of Jesus.
12. Every spirit of slumber, I bury you today, in the name of Jesus.
13. The eagle of my calling shall mount up by the power in the blood of Jesus.

14. Every anti-ministry arrow fired into my life, backfire, in the name of Jesus.

15. Holy Ghost fire, destroy all works of the devil in my life, in the name of Jesus.

16. Every door opened to the enemy of my calling, be closed, in the name of Jesus.

17. Let the waters of life, flow into every dead area of my spiritual life in the name of Jesus.

18. Every weapon fashioned against my high calling, be destroyed, in the name of Jesus.

19. Any foundational serpent and scorpion, programmed into my life to destroy my calling in future, die, in the Jesus' name

20. God of Elijah, arise and give me my mantle of fire, in the name of Jesus.

21. Anything planted within me that has not manifested now but will manifest in the future to make me backslide, dry up, in the name of Jesus.

22. Every witchcraft power drinking the blood of my spiritual life, die, in the name of Jesus.

23. Glory of God, overshadow me, in the name of Jesus.

24. Strength of God, empower me, in the name of Jesus.

25. Every internal bondage, magnetising external bondage, be broken, in the name of Jesus.

26. Glory of my calling, arise and shine, in the name of Jesus.

27. I will not mortgage my calling on the lap of Delilah and Jezebel, in the name of Jesus.

28. I refuse to retire. I must refire, in the name of Jesus.

29. Every enemy of my divine 'well done' at the end of my race, die, in the name of Jesus.
30. My Samson will not be shaven, in the name of Jesus.
31. I receive power to meet the needs of this present generation, in the name of Jesus.
32. All the rough places in my life targeted at my spiritual breakthroughs, be smoothened by the blood of Jesus.
33. Let Your glory, O Lord, overshadow my destiny, in the name of Jesus.
34. I refuse to tarry in the valley of powerlessness, in the name of Jesus.
35. I rise above my roots, by the power in the blood of Jesus.

DESTINY MARCHING ORDERS

YOU MUST MOVE FROM FEAR TO FAITH

You must move from fear to faith. Fear ruins destiny. Faith builds destiny. When your heart is filled with fear, the journey of destiny will become confusing. Fear is the destroyer of faith. The journey of destiny requires all the faith you can muster. To move from where you are and get to where God wants you to be, you need faith.

You need faith at the beginning of the journey of destiny. You need faith at the beginning of crucial projects as you pursue your destiny. You need faith midway on the journey of destiny. You need faith to believe God for the impossible. You need faith to address your mountain. You need faith to tackle the strongman who has vowed that the journey of your destiny will be truncated. If you must move forward in life faith must be your constant companion.

Remember that fear will force faith to jump out. The enemy will do everything to make you abandon your faith and celebrate your fear. The story of how Peter walked on the sea to go to Jesus reminds us of the conflict between fear and faith. Peter discovered his destiny when he saw Jesus Christ walking on the sea.

He began the journey of destiny by faith. Hardly had he gone a little distance when fear stepped in to distablise the journey. Immediately Peter embraced fear, his faith dropped from a great height and he began to sink.

Without faith the ship of your destiny will begin to sink. You must deal with fear. It must be banished from your heart. You must manifest ever increasing faith. Your faith must be consistent and fresh. You must keep on believing even when the evidence is contrary. The Bible tells us that faith is the substance of things hoped for.

Heb 11:1-3 says:
> *Now faith is the substance of things hoped for, the evidence of things not seen. For by it the elders obtained a good report. Through faith we understand that the worlds were framed by the word of God, so that things which are*

seen were not made of things which do appear.
Heb 11:1-3.

Without faith your destiny cannot be fulfilled. Manifest faith today and your destiny will receive fresh fire from above.

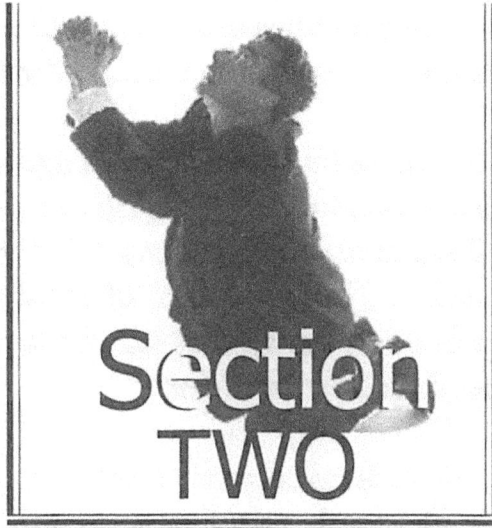

Section TWO

DESTINY CONFESSIONS

I am a stranger to fear. Because God has not given me the spirit of fear but of power and of a sound mind. My destiny has been established on the platform of faith. The Almighty has purged me of all negative encumbrances of fear. I overthrow the fear and the threats of the past. By faith I mount up with wings as an eagle. I leap over the walls of doubt and unbelief. My faith is waxing stronger by the day.

I therefore make bold to announce that greater is the One that is in me than any devil on the side of my enemies. It is written, *"The righteous is as bold as a lion."* By my faith in Christ Jesus I am righteous. I receive my divine boldness. "The angels of the Lord encampeth round about them that fear Him." The angels of the Lord are with me. I have no basis to fear any man, any evil or any foul-smelling spirit, because the Lord God of host is with me. I put my confidence and trust in God.

It is written, *"If God be for us, who can be against us?"* God is with me; I have no reason to fear, in the name of Jesus. It is written: *"The Lord is my light and my salvation, of whom shall I be afraid?... Though a host of evildoers encamp around me, my heart will not fear; though war rises against me, even in this I shall be confident."*

Satan and his world of demons cannot stand against me, because I am covered by the blood of the Lamb of God. And there is between me and the evil a standard of God raised with the Cross of Calvary by the Spirit of God. The Lord is with me like a mighty terrible One. I am not afraid. I cannot be threatened. My persecutors shall all stumble, fumble and fall. Their everlasting confusion and disgrace shall never be forgotten. God has commanded me to fear not, for He is in total control. Amen.

In the time of trouble, the Lord my God and my Father, shall hide me in his pavilion; in the secret places of His tabernacle shall He hide me. He shall set me upon a rock, and shall lift up my head above my enemies round about me. He shall tread down my enemies and render their camp desolate. For the rod of the wicked shall not rest upon the lot of the righteous. I am not afraid of the attack of the enemy, because it shall come to nothing. Nor am I afraid of the desolation of the wicked when it comes, for the Lord shall be my confidence and shall keep my foot from being taken.

Behold, all that are incensed against me shall be ashamed and confounded: they shall be as nothing; and they that strive with me shall perish. I shall seek them, and shall not find them, even they that contend with me. They that war against me shall be as nothing, and as a thing of nought. Behold, they surely gather together, but not by me: whosoever shall gather against me shall fall for my sake. The Lord shall deliver me in times of trouble. I shall not fall by the sword of the enemy. My enemies shall be like preys. The Lord shall avenge me and deliver me by the precious blood of His Lamb, Jesus Christ of Nazareth. Amen.

Section
THREE

DESTINY SCRIPTURES

Ah Lord GOD! behold, thou hast made the heaven and the earth by thy great power and stretched out arm, and there is nothing too hard for thee: Thou shewest lovingkindness unto thousands, and recompensest the iniquity of the fathers into the bosom of their children after them: the Great, the Mighty God, the LORD of hosts, is his name, Great in counsel, and mighty in work: for thine eyes are open upon all the ways of the sons of men: to give every one according to his ways, and according to the fruit of his doings: Which hast set signs and wonders in the land of Egypt, even unto this day, and in Israel, and among other men; and hast made thee a name, as at this day; And hast brought forth thy people Israel out of the land of Egypt with signs, and with wonders, and with a strong hand, and with a stretched out arm, and with great terror. Jer 32:17-21.

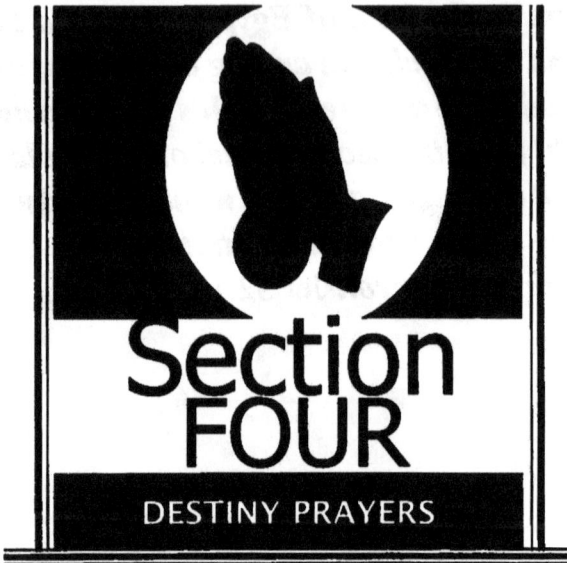

Section FOUR

DESTINY PRAYERS

Day 1

1. I bind and paralyse every strongman of fear in my life, in the name of Jesus.
2. I loose myself from the bondage of fear, in Jesus' name.
3. I loose myself from all negative religious fear, bondage to traditions of demons and men, religious images and witchcraft prophecies, in Jesus' name.
4. I loose myself from all demonic fears and from all their tormenting and enslaving powers, in Jesus' name.
5. I loose myself from every unholy fears of man, and I receive divine boldness, faith, confidence and inner strength, in Jesus' name.
6. Let all the entrances of fear into my life, be closed forever,

in the name of Jesus.

7. I plead the blood of Jesus over my heart, soul, spirit and body.

8. Let all the habitation of fear in my life be demolished, in Jesus' name

9. I bind every spirit of fear afflicting my life, in Jesus' name.

10. I render you spirit of fear of. . . (name them) powerless, in the name of Jesus.

11. I expel every spirit of fear in my life, in the name of Jesus.

12. Lord, break the bands of fear in my life.

13. Let all fears emanating from parental influence, past associations and guilt, depart from my spirit, in Jesus' name

14. I command the strongholds of fear to break, in Jesus' name.

15. You spirit of fear, I command you to come out of your hiding places and depart from my mind, my emotions, my will, my spirit and my body, in the name of Jesus.

16. Let all the problems introduced by fear into my life depart now, in the name of Jesus.

17. I stand against the spirit of fear of: (pick one by one): in the name of Jesus.

- air planes	- ambulances	- failure barbers
- other people's opinion		-future heights
- flying	- cats	- chicken
- people	- spiders	- cancer
- dogs	- water	
- demons	- insects	- marriage
- women	- robbers	- worms -
- blood	- sleep	- skin diseases

- ridicule   - mice   - corpses
- pregnancy   - insanity   - diseases
- crowds   - children   - poverty

Day 2

1. I command every spiritual contamination in my life to receive healing, in the name of Jesus.
2. Brush of the Lord, begin to scrub out every dirt in my spiritual pipe.
3. Every rusted pipe in my life, become new, in Jesus' name.
4. I command every power eating up my spiritual pipe to be roasted, in the name of Jesus.
5. I command every blockage in my spiritual pipe to be removed, in the name of Jesus.
6. I command the hole in my spiritual pipe to be closed, in the name of Jesus.
7. Let the heavenly plumber repair my spiritual pipe, in Jesus' name.
8. Let my spiritual pipe receive the strength of God against any contamination, in the name of Jesus.
9. I receive heavenly flushing in my spiritual pipe, in Jesus' name.
10. I confess that my spiritual pipe shall be effective throughout my life, in the name of Jesus.
11. Every evil padlock and every evil chain, go back to the senders, in the name of Jesus.
12. I rebuke every spirit of deafness and blindness in my life, in the name of Jesus.
13. I bind the strongman behind my spiritual blindness and deafness and I paralyse his operations in my life, in the

name of Jesus.

14. I anoint my eyes and my ears with the blood of Jesus.

15. Lord, restore my spiritual eyes and ears, in the name of Jesus.

16. Lord, anoint my eyes and my ears that they may see and hear.

17. I send the fire of God to my eyes and ears to melt away any satanic deposits, in the name of Jesus.

18. Spiritual eyes and ears, I command you in the name of Jesus, be opened, in the name of Jesus.

19. I capture, every power behind my spiritual blindness and deafness, in Jesus' name.

20. Let every blind spiritual sight and dead ear drum receive healing, in the name of Jesus.

21. You blind and deaf spirit, loose your hold over my life, in the name of Jesus.

22. I will not throw away, my gift of salvation, in the name of Jesus.

23. Let water of life, flush out every unwanted stranger in my life, in the name of Jesus.

24. You haters of God's salvation in my life, I command you to roast, in the name of Jesus.

25. You pollutants of life, I pollute you, in the name of Jesus.

26. Lord, put into my hand the gift that will elevate my life.

27. Holy Spirit fire, cook me to the glory of God, in the name of Jesus.

28. Lord, let the anointing of the Holy Spirit break every yoke of retrogression in my life, in the name of Jesus.

29. Let the blood of Jesus remove any unprogressive label from every aspect of my life, in the name of Jesus.
30. I reject the spirit of the tail, I choose the spirit of the head, in the name of Jesus.
31. I paralyse the ability of any demonic power limiting my progress, in the name of Jesus.

Day 3

1. Lord, give unto me the key to good success, so that anywhere I go the doors of good success will be opened unto me.
2. Lord, establish me as a holy person unto you, in Jesus' name.
3. Lord, let the anointing to excel in my spiritual and physical life fall on me, in the name of Jesus.
4. I declare with my mouth that nothing shall be impossible with me, in the name of Jesus.
5. I reject the anointing of non–achievement in my handiwork, in the name of Jesus.
6. Lord, let your favour and that of men encompass me this year, in the name of Jesus.
7. Holy Spirit, control my ability to frame my words.
8. Let scorpions be rendered harmless in every area of my life, in the name of Jesus.
9. Let serpents be rendered harmless in every area of my life, in the name of Jesus.
10. Let the camp of the enemy be put in disarray, in Jesus' name.
11. Let all my Herods receive spiritual decay, in the name of Jesus.
12. Let evil worms in any area of my life die, in the name of Jesus.

13. Let all handwritings against me be paralysed, in Jesus' name.
14. All those circulating my name for evil, be disgraced, in Jesus' name.
15. Let evil friends make mistakes that would expose them, in the name of Jesus.
16. Let the strongmen from both sides of my family destroy themselves, in the name of Jesus

DESTINY MARCHING ORDERS

YOU MUST MOVE FROM COMPLAINING TO OBTAINING

You must move from complaining to obtaining. The ability to fulfil your destiny in life depends on your attitude. God is able to do all things at all times. You can choose to manifest faith and possess your possessions. You can also choose to complain and murmur and manifest doubts and unbelief.

As you undertake the journey of destiny, you will surely come across challenging situations. These challenges will either make you to complain or to make use of the weapon of faith. You can complain from dawn to dusk and receive nothing from God. But you can go to the Almighty with faith and confidence and obtain grace at the hour of need.

Prayer is asking and receiving. You do not have to conquer God's reluctance as He is ever ready to do abundantly above what we ask. Those who murmur are telling God that they have no confidence in Him. But men and women of faith can turn their challenges to opportunities to obtain miracles and breakthroughs. When you are complaining and grumbling at all times, you will get nothing from God, for He has nothing to give to those who grumble and complain.

Those who grumbled in the wilderness died without getting to the Promise Land. But those who manifested faith got there. God is not in anyway bound to listen to your complaint. The only thing that can move Him is your faith. If you read Hebrews 11, you will discover the great exploits of the heroes of faith. None of them bagged mentioning by murmuring. They were rewarded because they moved from complaining to obtaining.

Read the exploits which they performed by obtaining true faith.

Heb 11:17-32:

> *By faith Abraham, when he was tried, offered up Isaac: and he that had received the promises offered up his only begotten son, Of whom it was said, That in Isaac shall thy seed be called: Accounting that God was able to raise him up, even from the dead; from whence also he received him in a figure. By faith Isaac blessed*

Jacob and Esau concerning things to come. By faith Jacob, when he was a dying, blessed both the sons of Joseph; and worshipped, leaning upon the top of his staff. By faith Joseph, when he died, made mention of the departing of the children of Israel; and gave commandment concerning his bones. By faith Moses, when he was born, was hid three months of his parents, because they saw he was a proper child; and they were not afraid of the king's commandment. By faith Moses, when he was come to years, refused to be called the son of Pharaoh's daughter; Choosing rather to suffer affliction with the people of God, than to enjoy the pleasures of sin for a season; Esteeming the reproach of Christ greater riches than the treasures in Egypt: for he had respect unto the recompence of the reward. By faith he forsook Egypt, not fearing the wrath of the king: for he endured, as seeing him who is invisible. Through faith he kept the passover, and the sprinkling of blood, lest he that destroyed the firstborn should touch them. By faith they passed through the Red sea as by dry land: which the Egyptians assaying to do were drowned. By faith the walls of Jericho fell down, after they were compassed about seven days. By faith the harlot Rahab perished not with them that believed not, when she had received the spies with peace. And what shall I more say? for the time would fail me to tell of Gedeon, and of Barak, and of Samson, and of Jephthae; of David also, and Samuel, and of the prophets.

You must convert murmuring to praying, complaining to obtaining and doubt to vibrant faith. If you manifest faith today, your destiny will attain unprecedented heights.

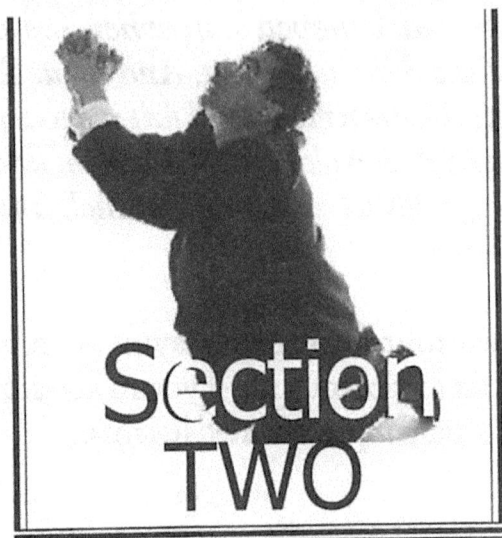

Section TWO

DESTINY CONFESSIONS

I am a new creation. I have a brand new life. My life is based on the principles of heaven. I am fashioned to reflect divine glory. God has opened my eyes to the realities of the new creation. I have come out of the camp of those who murmur and complain. I am not a slave. I am a bonafide beneficiary. God's rich, matchless and unlimited grace have been made available to me. I now have unfettered access to the overflowing storehouse of the Almighty. I have therefore moved from complaining to obtaining.

As a heir of God and joint heir with the Lord Jesus Christ, there is no room for murmuring or complaining in my life. My destiny is in God's hands. My God is able to do exceeding abundantly above all that I ask or think, according to the power that worketh in me. Therefore, I am divinely positioned to obtain my inheritance. God has prepared me for this new glorious era by giving me the priviledge of obtaining precious faith. God has given me exceeding great and precious promises that I might obtain favour, grace, power, anointing, prosperity, spiritual growth, divine benefits, promotion, accelerated progress, healing, health, victory in battles and every good and perfect gift which comes from above.

It is unrighteous for God to allow me to suffer in the midst of plenty. God means what He says and says what He means. His promises are sure. There is no variableness or shadow of turning with Him. Why then should I complain? Doors of blessings are already opened unto me. Strangers are submitting themselves unto me; therefore complaining is not part of my agenda. When others complain of poverty, I obtain prosperity. When others complain of failure, I obtain success. When others complain of being forgotten and isolated, I obtain favour or sudden divine attention. When others go through spiritual emptiness and dryness, I obtain fullness and freshness. When others are victims of circumstances, I emerge as someone who has obtained uncommon grace and is in control of circumstances.

Because the Lord has made me victorious, He shall also make me the head and not the tail. For greater is He who is in me, than he that is in the world. I shall be above only, and shall not be beneath. Because I fear the Lord, He shall bless me and encamp His holy angels round about me. The enemy shall fight against me with his troops, but they shall not prevail against me; "for I am with thee", saith the Lord, "to deliver thee".

The Lord God is good. He is my stronghold in the day of trouble; and He knoweth that I trust in Him with the whole of my heart, soul and spirit. With an overrunning flood will He make an utter end of my enemy's habitation. Darkness will pursue all my enemies, in the name of Jesus. I claim the power in the name of the Lord to overcome all the troops of the enemy. It is written that the Lord giveth power to the weak; He increases their strength. And those who wait on Him, He renews, enabling them to mount up with wings as eagles, to run and not be weary, to walk and not faint, to run over troops, to jump over walls and pass through fire without being hurt.

> *I am blessed because I trust in the Lord. I reverence the Lord, therefore is no want in my life. The young lions do lack and suffer hunger: but I shall not want any good things.* Psalm 34:8-10.

> *I have given and it shall be given unto me, good measure, pressed down, shaken together and running over, shall men give into my bosom. For with the same measure that I mete withal it shall be measured to me again.* Luke 9:8.

> *God is able to make all grace abound toward me, that I, always having all sufficiency in all things,*

may have an abundance for every good work. 2 Corn. 9:38.

I am prospering in every way. My body keeps well, even as my soul keeps well and prosper. 3 John 2.

Whatsoever I ask the Father in the name of Jesus His Son, He will give it to me. John 16:23.

Abraham's blessings are mine. Gal 3:14.

What things soever I desire, when I pray, I believe that I have received them and I shall have them. Mark 11:24.

I delight myself in the Lord, and He gives me the desires of my heart. Psalm 37:4.

I seek first the kingdom of God, therefore everything I need shall be added unto me. Luke 12:31.

Section
THREE

DESTINY SCRIPTURES

And Peter calling to remembrance saith unto him, Master, behold, the fig tree which thou cursedst is withered away. And Jesus answering saith unto them, Have faith in God. For verily I say unto you, That whosoever shall say unto this mountain, Be thou removed, and be thou cast into the sea; and shall not doubt in his heart, but shall believe that those things which he saith shall come to pass; he shall have whatsoever he saith. Therefore I say unto you, What things soever ye desire, when ye pray, believe that ye receive them, and ye shall have them. Mark 11:21-24.

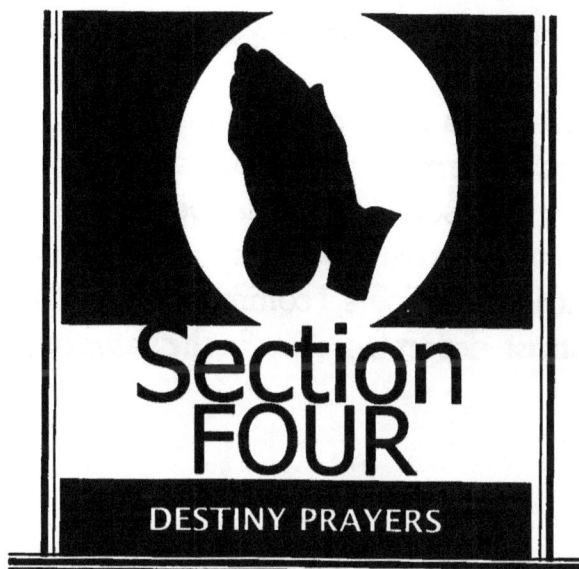

Section FOUR

DESTINY PRAYERS

Day 1

1. I cancel every conscious negative agreement, in Jesus' name.
2. Lord, make me Your battle axe, in the name of Jesus.
3. Let every spiritual weakness in my life receive termination now, in the name of Jesus.
4. Let every financial failure receive termination now, in the name of Jesus.
5. Let every sickness in my life receive termination, in the name of Jesus.
6. Let every architect of my problems receive termination now, in the name of Jesus.

7. I paralyse all spiritual wolves working against my life, in the name of Jesus.
8. Let that which hinders me from greatness begin to give way now, in the mighty name of Jesus.
9. Let every imprisoned and buried potential begin to come forth now, in the name of Jesus.
10. You unfriendly helpers, I command you, in the name of Jesus Christ, depart from me, in the name of Jesus.

Day 2

1. Let every negative transaction, currently affecting my life negatively, be cancelled, in the name of Jesus.
2. I command all the dark works done against my life in secret to be exposed and be nullified, in the name of Jesus.
3. I loose myself from any evil spirit, in the name of Jesus.
4. Lord, if my life is on the wrong course correct me, in the name of Jesus.
5. Let every anti-progress altar fashioned against me be destroyed with the thunder fire of God, in the name of Jesus.
6. I command my destiny to change to the best, in Jesus' name.
7. Let my hand become a sword of fire to cut down demonic trees, in the name of Jesus.
8. All boasting powers delegated against me, be silenced permanently, in the name of Jesus.
9. I withdraw all my benefits from the hands of the oppressors, in the name of Jesus.
10. Let all unprofitable marks in my life be erased, in Jesus' name.
11. Let every power chasing away my blessings be paralysed, in the name of Jesus.

12. Let every good thing eaten up by the enemy be vomited now, in the name of Jesus.   .

13. Let the anointing for spiritual breakthrough fall upon me, in the name of Jesus.

14. Lord, make me a prayer addict, in the name of Jesus.

15. Lord, ignite my prayer life with Your fire, in the name of Jesus.

16. Lord, empower my prayer altar, in the name of Jesus.

17. I reject every spiritual contamination, in the name of Jesus.

18. Lord, give me power to overcome all obstacles to my breakthroughs, in the name of Jesus.

19. Lord, give me divine prescription to my problems, in the name of Jesus.

20. I break all curses of leaking blessings, in the name of Jesus.

21. Let all spiritual holes in my life be closed with the blood of Jesus, in the name of Jesus.

22. Lord, help me to locate the defect in the clay of my life, in the name of Jesus.

23. Lord, let me be at the right place at the right time, in the name of Jesus.

24. I disarm every household enemy today, in the name of Jesus.

25. Let my enemies pitch their tents against one another, in the name of Jesus.

26. I frustrate and disappoint every instrument of the enemy fashioned against me, in the name of Jesus.

27. I seal my victory with the blood of Jesus.
28. I thank You Lord Jesus for answering my prayers.

Day 3

1. I receive the goodness of the Lord in the land of the living, in the name of Jesus.
2. Everything done against me to spoil my joy this year, be destroyed, in the name of Jesus.
3. Lord, as Abraham received favour in Your hands, let me receive Your favour so that I can excel, in the name of Jesus.
4. Lord Jesus, deal bountiful with me this year, in the name of Jesus.
5. It does not matter whether 1 deserve it or not, I receive unqualified favour from the Lord, in the name of Jesus.
6. Every blessing that God would distribute this year will not pass me by, in the name of Jesus.
7. My blessing will not be transferred to my neighbour, in the name of Jesus.
8. Father Lord, disgrace every power that is out to steal Your programme for my life, in the name of Jesus.
9. Every step that I take this year shall lead to outstanding success, in the name of Jesus.
10. I shall prevail with man and with God, in the name of Jesus
11. Spend quality time to bless the name of the Lord.

DESTINY MARCHING ORDERS

YOU MUST MOVE FROM DRIFTING TO BEING STEADY

If you must fulfill your destiny, you must avoid anything that looks like drifting. Those who make it in life do not move from one place to the other like butterflies. Slow and steady, they say, wins the race. The journey of destiny must be steady and consistent. You must not be in doubt concerning what constitutes your destination. If God has destined you to become a great success through the use of human skills, you cannot afford to veer off from your calling or destiny and begin to drift as if you had no aim.

The secret of success, as far as destiny is concerned, is focus. The journey of destiny may take you a long time, but your slow and steady steps will take you there. One of the powers which you must address is the power of drifting. When the enemy succeeds in making you to drift, you will be left with little or no time to pursue your destiny.

It is crystal clear that your destiny is your major pre-occupation in life. Your destiny is what God sent you to this world to achieve. It is the particular thing you can do in a unique manner. It is a product of your gifts and endowment. It is your peculiar bus stop. It is the divine agenda for your life. It is your number one assignment as you sojourn in this world.

Therefore, you cannot pursue your destiny by becoming a jack of all trades and master of none. God Has created you for a purpose. It is never part of His agenda that you drift from one place to another. There are people who have tried their hands on various things by drifting from the work of a cobbler to that of an auto mechanic. Some have also gone from doing business to setting up a school without any purpose.

Those who drift hardly achieve any meaningful thing. You must go from drifting to taking up the steering of your destiny in a calculated manner. It is time to take the steering wheel of your destiny from the devil and steer your destiny back to where God wants it to be.

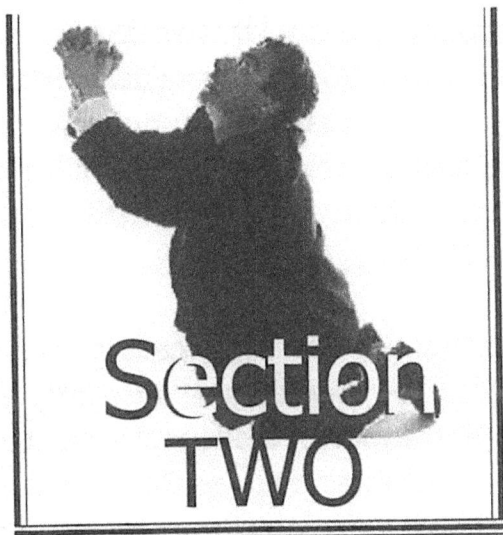

SECTION TWO

DESTINY CONFESSIONS

I am a product of perfect divine design. My destiny is not an accident. It is fashioned at Heaven's workshop. I refuse to drift. I have resolved to live a purposeful life. I am not a vagrant. I am committed to God's purpose for my life and destiny. I have already said goodbye to drifting. Since my times are in God's hands, my progress will be steady. He has given meaning to my life. I know who I am. I know where I am heading to. Others may drift but I cannot. Others may erect their buildings of destiny on platforms that are shaky, I cannot.

I am not an aimless wonderer, I am not moving from pillar to post like others. My goal is clear. My purpose is sealed. My destination has been clearly spelt out. I am moving forward.

God has not brought me this far to make me drift like a ship captured by the storm. My destiny is anchored to the poles of the Almighty. The storms of life cannot shake me. I refuse to go through life blindly. I reject the agenda of moving in circles as if blindfolded. From now on, the lines shall fall unto me in pleasant places. I have a godly heritage.

Heaven is maintaining the lot of my destiny. Every programme will fall into place. My success shall be steady. My goals and aspirations shall be achieved. God has attached to me angels on assignment, whose duties are to ensure that I make it in life. I am not an abandoned project. I am not a factory defect. My destiny is not a mistake. The details of my destiny are written on the palms of the Almighty. The spirit of God has given me all the backing necessary to make it to the top. Heaven has charted a glorious pathway for me. God has gone ahead to make all crooked places straight for me. My life, will hence forth remain a perfect example of how God can make the impossible possible.

Therefore, accelerated progress, steady success and unprecedented breakthroughs shall envelope my destiny. Kings shall nourish me. Strangers shall submit themselves unto me. The yoke of darkness shall not stand in my life. God Has imbued me with the strength of an unicorn. I shall walk steadily unto the top and my story shall change for the best to the glory of God.

I am a child of God. I am dwelling in the secret place of the most high God. I am protected and covered under the shadow of the wings of Jehovah, in Jesus' name. Amen

The word of God is the power of God, and the entrance of the word of God into my life has brought the light of God into my life, and darkness cannot comprehend it, in Jesus' name. I send forth this light that is in me as a two-edged sword to destroy all the kingdoms of darkness, in Jesus' name. Amen.

The word of God is quick and powerful in my mouth. God has put the power of His word in my mouth, in Jesus' name. I trust the word of God. The word stands sure when I speak it. When I speak it, it will accomplish the purpose for which I have spoken it, in Jesus' name. Amen.

My strength is in the Lord Jesus Christ. Jesus is my strength, I receive strength from Him, in Jesus' name. Amen.

There is no weakness in me, for I have received the might of God. I am strong. I can do all things through Christ who strengthens me. I walk and I do not faint, I run and I am not weary, in Jesus' name. Amen.

The Spirit of Christ that dwells inside me strengthens my physical body, in Jesus' name. Amen.

I have prayer power, in Jesus' name. Amen.

I pray without ceasing. I am fortified with the strength to pray, in Jesus' name. Amen.

Jesus Christ has given me His peace and I receive it, in Jesus' name. Amen

I have the peace of God that surpasses all understanding. It keeps my heart and keeps my mind through Christ Jesus, in Jesus' name. Amen.

My mind is renewed by the word of God day by day, in Jesus' name. Amen.

Section
THREE

DESTINY SCRIPTURES

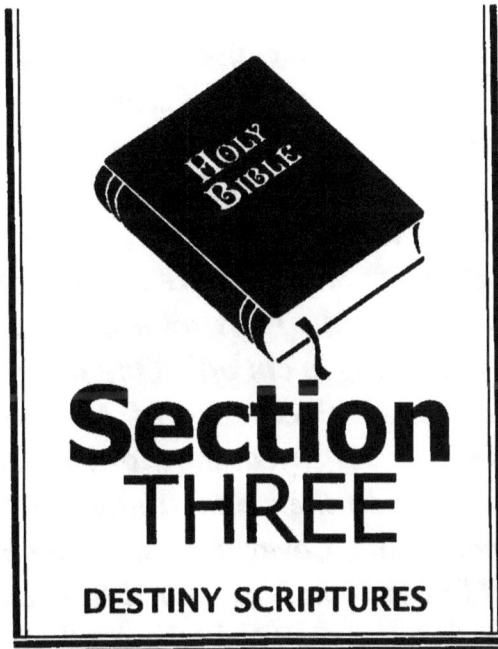

Israel is an empty vine, he bringeth forth fruit unto himself: according to the multitude of his fruit he hath increased the altars; according to the goodness of his land they have made goodly images. Their heart is divided; now shall they be found faulty: he shall break down their altars, he shall spoil their images. For now they shall say, We have no king, because we feared not the LORD; what then should a king do to us? They have spoken words, swearing falsely in making a covenant: thus judgment springeth up as hemlock in the furrows of the field. The inhabitants of

Samaria shall fear because of the calves of Beth-aven: for the people thereof shall mourn over it, and the priests thereof that rejoiced on it, for the glory thereof, because it is departed from it. It shall be also carried unto Assyria for a present to king Jareb: Ephraim shall receive shame, and Israel shall be ashamed of his own counsel. As for Samaria, her king is cut off as the foam upon the water. The high places also of Aven, the sin of Israel, shall be destroyed: the thorn and the thistle shall come up on their altars; and they shall say to the mountains, Cover us; and to the hills, Fall on us. O Israel, thou hast sinned from the days of Gibeah: there they stood: the battle in Gibeah against the children of iniquity did not overtake them. It is in my desire that I should chastise them; and the people shall be gathered against them, when they shall bind themselves in their two furrows. And Ephraim is as an heifer that is taught, and loveth to tread out the corn; but I passed over upon her fair neck: I will make Ephraim to ride; Judah shall plow, and Jacob shall break his clods. Sow to yourselves in righteousness, reap in mercy; break up your fallow ground: for it is time to seek the LORD, till he come and rain righteousness upon you. Hos 10:1-12.

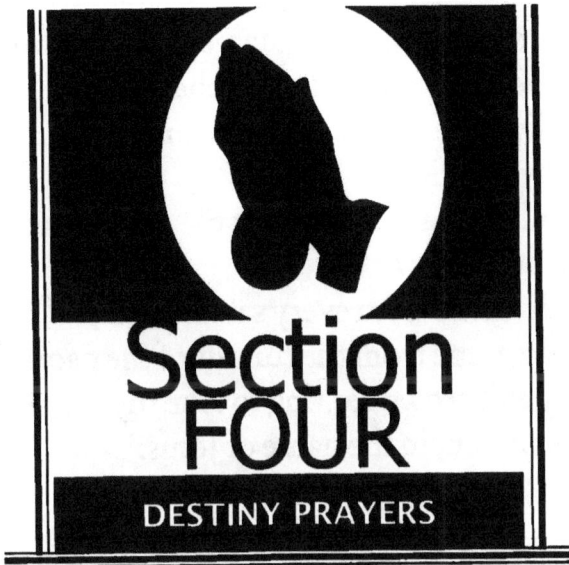

Section FOUR

DESTINY PRAYERS

Day 1

1. You powers that quench the fire of God in one's life, I am not your candidate, in the name of Jesus.
2. Every deeply rooted problem in my life, be uprooted by fire, in the name of Jesus.
3. I reject every evil domination and bondage in my life, in the name of Jesus.
4. My angel of blessings will locate me today, in the name of Jesus
5. My angel of blessings will not go unless he blesses me, in the name of Jesus.
6. Lord, let my cries provoke angelic assistance today.
7. Lord, give me the name that would bless me today.

8. Let every satanic hindrance targeted against my angel of blessing be dissolved by fire, in the name of Jesus.
9. Lord, deliver me from evil stones thrown at me by unfriendly friends.
10. Every evil riot and rage against me, be disgraced, in Jesus' name.
11. Lord, deliver me from every satanic noise.
12. Lord, deliver me from the tumult of the people.
13. Let every evil crowd seeking to take my life be scattered unto desolation, in the name of Jesus.

Day 2

1. O Lord, bless me to a dumbfounding degree.
2. O Lord, enlarge my coast.
3. Let every embargo on my progress fall down and scatter, in the name of Jesus..
4. I reject satanic restrictions in every area of my life, in the name of Jesus.
5. Let the mighty hands of God be upon me for good, in Jesus' name.
6. Lord, keep me from all evil wisdom and manipulation.
7. I reject any invitation to appointment with sorrow, in Jesus' name.
8. I scatter evil multitudes gathered against me, in the name of Jesus.
9. Let God be God against my oppressors, in the name of Jesus.
10. The Lord will not be a spectator in my affairs but a participant, in the name of Jesus.
11. Lord, save me from sinking in the sea of life.
12. My head will not be anchored to doubt, in the name of Jesus.
13. I refuse any evil diversion, in the name of Jesus.
14. I will not take my eyes off the Lord Jesus, in the name of Jesus.
15. Lord, anchor your mercy to my head.

16. Lord Jesus, let me receive the touch of signs and wonders now.
17. Let God be God in my Red Sea situation, in the name of Jesus.
18. God, let it be known that You are God in every department of my life, in the name of Jesus.
19. Lord, do a new thing to my enemies that would permanently dismantle their power.

Day 3

1. Every attempt being made by destiny killers against my destiny, be frustrated unto death, in the name of Jesus.
2. I command the fire of God to come upon destiny killers working against my destiny, in the name of Jesus.
3. I remove my destiny from the camp of destiny killers, in the name of Jesus.
4. I use the fire of God and the blood of Jesus to surround my destiny, in the name of Jesus.
5. Every power working against the fruitfulness of my destiny, be disgraced, in the name of Jesus
6. I command my destiny to reject every bewitchment, in the name of Jesus.
7. I deliver my destiny from the grip of destiny killers, in Jesus' name.
8. Every evil done to my destiny by household wickedness, be reversed now, in the name of Jesus.
9. Every vessel of destiny killers fashioned against my destiny, fall down and die, in the name of Jesus.
10. Let the ground open now and swallow all destiny killers working against me, in the name of Jesus.
11. Every evil gathering against my destiny, scatter, in the name of Jesus.
12. My destiny, you will not manage poverty, in the name of Jesus.

13. My destiny, you will not manage failure, in the name of Jesus.
14. I command my destiny to begin to change to the best now, in the name of Jesus.
15. My head will not carry evil load, in the name of Jesus.
16. Every enemy of progress in my life, fall down and die now, in the name of Jesus.
17. I reject every evil manipulation against my destiny in every area of my life, in the name of Jesus.
18. I paralyse, every activity of destiny killers in every area of my life, in the name of Jesus.

DESTINY MARCHING ORDERS

YOU MUST MOVE FROM BEING A PROBLEM TO BEING AN ANSWER

The major reason why many destinies have remained in the dustbin of failure is that many people have remained experts at parading their problems. The majority of people on earth are busy complaining of one problem or the other. Many are busy nursing and cherishing their problems. Only very few have graduated from the school of problems. People who have become answers to people's problems are scarce. The ratio of problem solvers to those who are weighed down by their problems, has reached an optimum level. If all you know how to do is to complain about your problems or project your challenges, you are far from the realm of destiny fulfillment.

You must get to a point where you become an answer to the problems of many people around you. Jesus is our perfect example. The Bible tells us that He went about doing good. He was busy solving human problems. You cannot maximise your potential if you are busy murmuring and licking old wounds. You must stand tall and come up with the destiny of a problem solver.

You can become the Moses of your generation. You can become the Joshua of this generation. You can be used by God as the Joseph who would save many people from perishing. You must pray until you locate the positive values within you. To fulfill your destiny you must get to a point where you are able to explore your potentials maximally.

Wherever you find yourself in a group do not be an Achan. You must pray until you become a divine arrow-head to your generation. You must fulfill your destiny by functioning as a problem solver tothe multitudes around you. This can only take place through aggressive prayers.

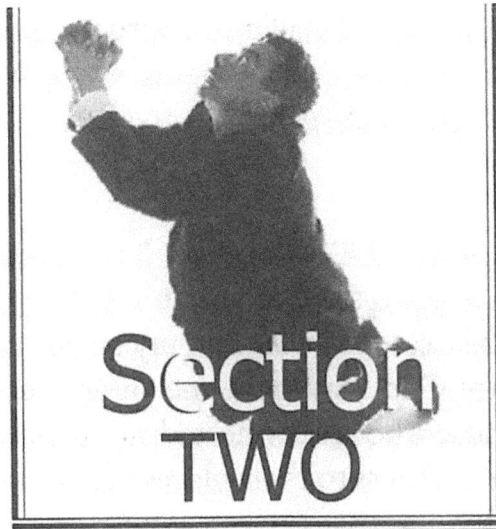

Section TWO

DESTINY CONFESSIONS

I have a unique destiny. I do not live my life in the realm of problems. I am not a problem but an answer to people's problems. I am aware of the fact that a lot of people's destinies are attached to my own destiny. Hence I am a problem solver and not a problem. I am a burden bearer and not a burden. I am a pathfinder and not a confused traveler on the highway of life. God Has made me an answer to the hopes, yearnings and aspirations of millions of people.

God has made my tongue the pen of a ready writer. I speak hope to the hopeless, peace to the troubled and progress to the backward. I shall not live in the dark, since I am the light of the world. I shall diffuse darkness. Wherever I find disturbing questions, I shall give answers of peace. Wherever people are languishing in the valley, I shall move unto the mountain top. I am God's battle axe. I am God's weapon of war. With me, God shall break into pieces the iron bars and destroy the cages of darkness.

I am an instrument of God's peace. I am a fore-runner of goodness. I am a stepping stone to people's divine breakthroughs. Since my speech is seasoned with salt, my hearers shall savour a good taste. Since God Has made me an answer to people's problems, all those who are connected to me shall move from the dungeon of darkness to their places of rest and freedom.

God has not created me to nurture personal problems; neither has He made me to grapple with setbacks, discouragement and apathy. My God has deposited in my life not only what I need to overcome my own problems but also endowed me with the machinery, that will produce specific answers to specific problems of people. My tongue shall speak peace. My nose shall breathe success. My life shall exemplify God's rich and matchless grace. My destiny shall prove to all and sundry that Jesus is the answer to all problems of mankind.

Therefore, I receive creative ideas which will feed multitudes. I receive the wisdom of a comforting counsellor to all who shall come to me. God has connected me with enough financial resources to meet the needs of multitudes which have no means of survival. The Spirit of God shall give me the right word whenever I open my mouth to answer people's questions. Since

God has made me unique, I shall be a source of encouragement to those who are tired of their existence. The anointing of God upon my life shall produce answers which will transform many people's destinies. As I move from being a problem to being an answer, I shall make positive history and emerge as someone who has been set up by God to be a destiny moulder.

Right now, I stand in my position as a true child of Jehovah God, ordained to reign as a king on earth, and I command the flavour of divine favour of God to fill me. God has put His word in my mouth as a weapon of destruction and restoration. I use that power to speak destruction upon all devil's agents assigned to hinder me and divert my blessings. I use the same weapon to decree restoration upon my life. It is written that I should discard the former things. God shall do a new thing in my life and it shall spring forth. Now, I decree that new things begin to spring forth in my marriage, in my business, in my finances and in my spiritual life.

The Lord will make His face to shine upon me always and shall be gracious unto me. His light will shine on my path and His favour will encompass me all the days of my life.

I cover my confessions with the precious blood of the Lamb of God, in the name of Jesus.

Section
THREE

DESTINY SCRIPTURES

And the LORD said, I have surely seen the affliction of my people which are in Egypt, and have heard their cry by reason of their taskmasters; for I know their sorrows; And I am come down to deliver them out of the hand of the Egyptians, and to bring them up out of that land unto a good land and a large, unto a land flowing with milk and honey; unto the place of the Canaanites, and the Hittites, and the Amorites, and the Perizzites, and the Hivites, and the Jebusites. Now therefore, behold, the cry of the children of Israel is come unto me: and I have also seen the oppression wherewith the Egyptians oppress them.

Come now therefore, and I will send thee unto Pharaoh, that thou mayest bring forth my people the children of Israel out of Egypt. And Moses said unto God, Who am I, that I should go unto Pharaoh, and that I should bring forth the children of Israel out of Egypt? And he said, Certainly I will be with thee; and this shall be a token unto thee, that I have sent thee: When thou hast brought forth the people out of Egypt, ye shall serve God upon this mountain. Ex. 3:7-12.

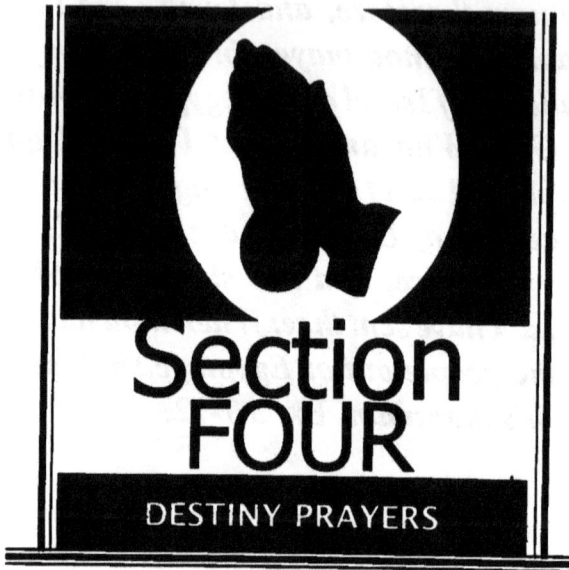

Section FOUR

DESTINY PRAYERS

Day 1

1. Every incantation, ritual and witchcraft power against my destiny, fall down and die, in the name of Jesus.
2. I render null and void the influence of destiny swallowers, in the name of Jesus.
3. Every household wickedness struggling to re-arrange my destiny, fall down and die, in the name of Jesus.
4. My destiny is attached to God, therefore, I decree that I can never fail, in the name of Jesus.
5. I refuse to be programmed against my divine destiny in the name of Jesus.
6. I destroy every record of my destiny in the marine world,

in the name of Jesus.
7.   Every altar mounted against my destiny in the heavenlies, be dismantled, in the name of Jesus.
8.   I reject every satanic alternative for my destiny, in Jesus' name.
9.   Evil caldrons, you will not cook up my destiny, in Jesus' name.
10.   I destroy every witchcraft caldron and concoction against my destiny, in the name of Jesus.
11.   Every power of the caldron raised up to manipulate my destiny, release me, in the name of Jesus.
12.   Destiny swallowers, vomit my destiny, in the name of Jesus.
13.   I recover my stolen vehicle of destiny, in the name of Jesus.
14.   Every conference of darkness against my destiny, scatter, in the name of Jesus.
15.   Lord, anoint my destiny afresh.
16.   Failure shall not slaughter my destiny, in the name of Jesus.
17.   Every power waging war against my destiny, fall down and die, in the name of Jesus.
18.   Destiny thieves, release me now, in the name of Jesus.
19.   I overthrow every satanic re-arrangement programmed against my destiny, in the name of Jesus.

Day 2

1. I have come to Zion, my destiny must change, in Jesus' name.
2. Every power derailing my destiny, fall down and die, in the name of Jesus.
3. I refuse to miss my destiny in life, in the name of Jesus.
4. I refuse to accept satanic substitute for my destiny, in the name of Jesus.
5. Anything programmed against my destiny in the heavenlies, be shaken down, in the name of Jesus.
6. Every power drawing power from the heavenlies against my destiny, fall down and die, in the name of Jesus.
7. Every satanic altar fashioned against my destiny, fall down and die, in the name of Jesus.
8. Lord, take away my destiny from the hands of men.
9. I revoke every satanic ownership on my destiny, in Jesus' name.
10. Satan, you will not settle down on my destiny, in Jesus' name.
11. My destiny shall not suffer affliction, in the name of Jesus.
12. Every association of emptier against my destiny, scatter by the word of God, in the name of Jesus.
13. Today, I raise up an altar of continuous prosperity upon my destiny, in the name of Jesus.
14. You anchor of failure keeping down my destiny, break, in the name of Jesus.
15. Every evil bank, established against my destiny, be liquidated by fire, in the name of Jesus.

16. I pronounce judgement against every evil altar erected against my destiny, in the name of Jesus.

17. Let my divine destiny appear, let my perverted destiny disappear, in the name of Jesus.

18. I reject every satanic re-arrangement of my destiny, in the name of Jesus.

19. Every evil power with the awareness of my destiny, be impotent, in the name of Jesus.

20. I paralyse every destiny polluter, in the name of Jesus.

Day 3

1. Every damage done to my destiny, be repaired, in Jesus' name.
2. The enemy will not convert my destiny to rags, in Jesus' name.
3. Lord, lay Your hands of fire and change upon my destiny.
4. I reject and renounce destiny demoting names and nullify their evil effects upon my destiny, in Jesus' name.
5. Any evil record against my destiny in the heavenlies as a result of destiny-demoting names, be wiped off, by the blood of Jesus.
6. I refuse to operate below my divine destiny, in Jesus' name.
7. Every power contending with my divine destiny, scatter, in the name of Jesus.
8. Lord, change my destiny to the best that will dumbfound my enemies.
9. Satan, I resist and rebuke your efforts to change my destiny, in the name of Jesus.
10. Satan, I remove from you the right to rob me of my divine destiny, in the name of Jesus.
11. I command all powers of darkness assigned to my destiny, to leave and never to return, in the name of Jesus.
12. The desire of my enemy against my destiny will not be granted in the heavenlies, in the name of Jesus.
13. The designs of my enemy against my destiny shall be destroyed, in the name of Jesus.

DESTINY MARCHING ORDERS

YOU MUST MOVE FROM GIVING EXCUSES TO BEING COMMITTED

The greatest problem in the area of destiny is that many are not ready to stick out their necks. Many people give excuses, even without understanding their assignment. God is ready to give us lots of assignments in the area of destiny, but we drag our feet by giving excuses. We either look at the sky and blame the cloud for making it impossible to perform our God given duties or we might even lay the blame on sunshine. Some people, go as far as saying that they cannot move out and fulfil their destiny because there is a lion in the street. But the truth is that as far as the land of destiny fulfilment is concerned excuse makers will be excused.

It is quite easy to give excuses, but it takes determination to climb the ladder of commitment. Everybody can give excuses but God is calling for those who would commit themselves and move ahead when others are resting on their oars. God had a great assignment for Moses. Even before he could understand the gravity of the assignment, he had come up with a litany of excuses. Unknown to Moses, he had been a child of destiny. God had preserved his life when he would have died, when all the first born were slaughtered. He did not know that he had a date with destiny. God wanted him to be a leader of the exodus from Egypt, but he busied himself with the task of leading animals in the bush.

Exodus 3:1 says:

Now Moses kept the flock of Jethro his father in law, the priest of Midian: and he led the flock to the backside of the desert, and came to the mountain of God, even to Horeb.

God had to use a mighty fire in the bush to arrest his attention.

According to Exodus 3:2-4:

And the angel of the LORD appeared unto him in a flame of fire out of the midst of a bush: and he looked, and, behold, the bush burned with fire, and the bush was not consumed. And Moses said, I will now turn aside, and see this great sight, why the bush is not burnt. And when the LORD saw that he turned aside to see, God called unto him out of the midst of the bush, and said, Moses, Moses. And he said, Here am I.

God gave Moses an assignment

Exodus 3:6-10 says:

Moreover he said, I am the God of thy father, the God of Abraham, the God of Isaac, and the God of Jacob. And Moses hid his face; for he was afraid to look upon God. And the LORD said, I have surely seen the affliction of my people which are in Egypt, and have heard their cry by reason of their taskmasters; for I know their sorrows; And I am come down to deliver them out of the hand of the Egyptians, and to bring them up out of that land unto a good land and a large, unto a land flowing with milk and honey; unto the place of the Canaanites, and the Hittites, and the Amorites, and the Perizzites, and the Hivites, and the Jebusites. Now therefore, behold, the cry of the children of Israel is come unto me: and I have also seen the oppression wherewith the Egyptians oppress them. Come now therefore, and I will send thee unto Pharaoh, that thou mayest bring forth my people the children of Israel out of Egypt.

He gave excuses. Exodus 3:11 says:

And Moses said unto God, Who am I, that I should go unto Pharaoh, and that I should bring forth the children of Israel out of Egypt?

He even told God that nobody would believe him and God had to perform mighty miracles to convince him.

Exodus 4:1-7:

And Moses answered and said, But, behold, they will not believe me, nor hearken unto my voice: for they will say, The LORD hath not appeared unto thee. And the LORD said unto him, What is that in thine hand? And he said, A rod. And he said, Cast it on the ground. And he cast it on the ground, and it became a serpent; and Moses fled from before it. And the LORD said unto Moses, Put forth thine hand, and take it by the tail. And he put forth his hand, and caught it, and it became a rod in his hand: That they may believe that the LORD God of their fathers, the God of Abraham, the God of Isaac, and the God of Jacob, hath appeared unto thee. And the LORD said furthermore unto him, Put now thine hand into thy bosom. And he put his hand into his bosom: and when he took it out, behold, his hand was leprous as snow. And he said, Put thine hand into thy bosom again. And he put his hand into his bosom again; and plucked it out of his bosom, and, behold, it was turned again as his other flesh.

He became convinced but still came up with an excuse that his speech impediment would not allow him to fulfil his destiny.

Exodus 4:10-14 says:

> *And Moses said unto the LORD, O my Lord, I am not eloquent, neither heretofore, nor since thou hast spoken unto thy servant: but I am slow of speech, and of a slow tongue. And the LORD said unto him, Who hath made man's mouth? or who maketh the dumb, or deaf, or the seeing, or the blind? have not I the LORD? Now therefore go, and I will be with thy mouth, and teach thee what thou shalt say. And he said, O my Lord, send, I pray thee, by the hand of him whom thou wilt send. And the anger of the LORD was kindled against Moses, and he said, Is not Aaron the Levite thy brother? I know that he can speak well. And also, behold, he cometh forth to meet thee: and when he seeth thee, he will be glad in his heart.*

At the end, Moses moved from excuses to uncommon commitment. By the time he stood in the courts of Pharaoh, it became clear to him that he had a great mandate from heaven. You need to stop giving excuses and take up your divine assignment, then you will be able to fulfil your destiny.

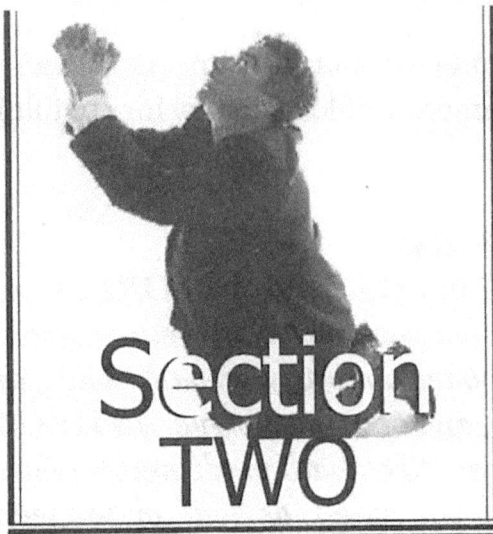

Section TWO

DESTINY CONFESSIONS

God has given me a new purpose and a new resolve to live gloriously. The resources of Heaven have been sufficiently deposited into my life that there is no room for excuses. I am not an excuse maker. I refuse to grumble or find excuses for failing in my responsibility. By the power of the Holy Spirit I am living on the positive side of life. I am aware of my divine responsibilities. God's agenda for my life is well known to me. I am not a carbon copy of anyone. I am an original. Of all the billions of people on the face of the earth there is no single person who looks exactly like me.

God has given me talents, abilities and specialised intelligence to make me function in the capacity He has placed me. No devil from the pit of hell can make me to give excuses. I do not lack anything. I am gifted and blessed. Where God wants me to function as the head I do not lack leadership qualities. Where God wants me to function as a positive example, I do not lack good exemplary qualities. Where God wants me to make sacrifice that can make a difference, I do not lack such qualities. Where God wants me to be a model of consecration and commitment, I do not lack such qualities.

I have decided to fulfill my place in destiny, since I know that things cannot be the same if I fail to fulfill my destiny. I have chosen to thread the path of commitment. I am resolved to be the best I can be. My carriage and comportment shall exude commitment. Where others complain I shall show commitment. I am committed to God, to the fulfillment of my destiny and to helping others fulfill their destinies.

Having been created in God's own image and justified by the finished work of Christ on the Cross of Calvary, I cherish the finished work of Christ on the Cross of Calvary, I cherish the fact of being a co-heir with Christ and all His divine possessions. By this has God blessed me with all heavenly blessings and seated me with Christ Jesus far above heavenly places.

Because I am the apple of God's eyes, He will this day set me over the nations and over the kingdoms, to root out, pull down, destroy, throw down, build and to plant. This very moment has God pulled down the strongholds of the enemy. He has planted me and given me power to tread upon serpents and scorpions and over all the power of the enemy; and nothing shall by any means hurt me.

It is written, "And the great dragon was cast out, that old serpent, called the devil, and satan, which decieveth the whole world; he was cast out into the earth, and his angels were cast out with him. And I heard a loud voice saying in Heaven, now is come salvation, and strength, and the kingdom of our God, and the power of His Christ; for the accuser of our brethren is cast down, which accused them before our God day and night."

With my heart I believe God, I believe His word, and I confess with my mouth that He is Jehovah God, who created the heaven and the earth. I confess that He is the beginning and the end of all things. He was, He is and forever shall be. With God, I believe nothing shall be impossible. God has spoken once and twice I have heard this, that all powers in heaven and on earth belong to Him.

As I say this prayer and confess the word of God, I command the spirits of distraction and hindrance to be bound, in the name of Jesus, I cast away from me every spirit of tiredness, weakness and defeat. In the mighty name of Jesus Christ, I command every knee of things in heaven, in the earth and in the seas that are against me, and these confessions, to bow and be bound.

Section
THREE

DESTINY SCRIPTURES

And Moses answered and said, But, behold, they will not believe me, nor hearken unto my voice: for they will say, The LORD hath not appeared unto thee. And the LORD said unto him, What is that in thine hand? And he said, A rod. And he said, Cast it on the ground. And he cast it on the ground, and it became a serpent; and Moses fled from before it. And the LORD said unto Moses, Put forth thine hand, and take it by the tail. And he put forth his hand, and caught it, and it became a rod in his hand: That they may believe that the LORD God of their fathers, the God of Abraham, the God of Isaac, and the God of Jacob, hath appeared unto thee. And the LORD said furthermore unto him, Put now thine hand into thy bosom. And he put his hand into his bosom: and when he took it out, behold, his hand was leprous as snow. And he said, Put thine hand into thy bosom again. And he put his hand into his bosom again; and plucked it out of his bosom, and, behold, it was turned again as his other flesh. And it shall come to pass, if they will not believe thee, neither hearken to the voice of the first sign, that they will believe the voice of the latter sign. And it shall come to pass, if they will not believe also these two signs, neither hearken unto thy voice, that thou shalt take of the water of the river, and pour it upon the dry land: and the water which thou takest out of the river shall become blood upon the dry land. And Moses said unto the LORD, O my Lord, I am not eloquent, neither heretofore, nor since thou hast spoken unto thy servant: but I am slow of speech, and of a slow tongue. And the LORD said unto him, Who hath made man's mouth? or who maketh the dumb, or deaf, or the seeing, or the blind? have not I the LORD? Now therefore go, and I will be with thy mouth, and teach thee what thou shalt say. Ex 4:1-12.

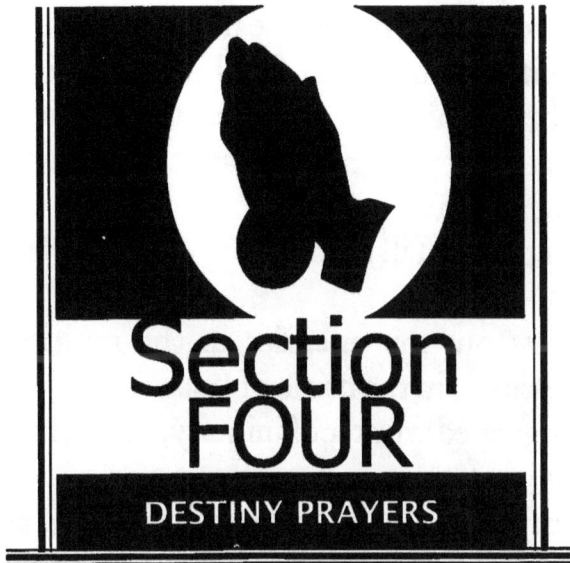

Section FOUR

DESTINY PRAYERS

Day 1

1. Let the rage of the wicked against me be rendered impotent, in the name of Jesus.
2. Let the imagination of the wicked against me be neutralized, in the name of Jesus.
3. Every counsel of evil kings against me, scatter, in the name of Jesus.
4. God, arise and speak in great wrath against the enemy of my breakthroughs, in the name of Jesus.
5. Every band of the wicked arresting my progress, break, in the name of Jesus.
6. Every cord of darkness militating against my breakthroughs, die, in the name of Jesus.
7. I will not be afraid, of 10,000 of people that have set

themselves against me, in the name of Jesus.

8. God, smite my enemies at the cheekbones, in Jesus' name.

9. My Father, break the teeth of the ungodly, in Jesus' name.

10. God, visit every power lying against me with destruction, in the name of Jesus.

11. Let my enemies fall by their own counsel, in the name of Jesus.

12. Lord, cast out my enemies in the multitude of their transgressions, in the name of Jesus.

13. Every organised worker of iniquity, depart from me, in the name of Jesus.

14. Let all my enemies be ashamed and sore vexed, in Jesus' name.

15. Let sudden shame be the lot of all my oppressors, in Jesus' name.

16. Every power planning to tear my soul like a lion, be dismantled, in the name of Jesus.

17. Let the wickedness of the wicked come to an end, O Lord, in the name of Jesus. .

18. God, prepare the instruments of death against my enemies, in the name of .Jesus.

19. God, ordain Your arrows against my persecutors, in the name of Jesus.

Day 2

1. Let every pit dug by the enemy become a grave for the enemy, in the name of Jesus.
2. I render null and void the effect of any interaction with satanic agents moving around as men, in the name of Jesus.
3. I pull down the stronghold of evil strangers in every area of my life, in the name of Jesus.
4. Any negative transaction currently affecting my life negatively, be cancelled, in the name of Jesus.
5. I command all the dark works done against me in secret to be exposed and nullified, in the name of Jesus.
6. I loose myself from the bondage of any dark spirit, in the name of Jesus.
7. Let all incantations against me be cancelled, in the name of Jesus.
8. I command all oppressors to retreat and flee in defeat, in the name of Jesus
9. I bind every strongman having my goods in his possession, in the name of Jesus.
10. I break the curse of automatic failure working upon my life, in the name of Jesus.
11. Let the anointing to prosper, fall mightily upon me now, in the name of Jesus.

Day 3

1. Thank God for making provision for deliverance from any form of bondage.
2. I release myself from any inherited bondage, in the name of Jesus.
3. I release myself from the grip of any problem transferred into my life from the womb, in the name of Jesus.
4. I break and loose myself from every inherited evil covenant, in the name of Jesus.
5. I break and loose myself from every inherited evil curse, in the name of Jesus.
6. I release myself from every inherited disease, in the name of Jesus.
7. Let the blood of Jesus correct any inherited defect in my body, in the name of Jesus.
8. In the name of Jesus, I break any curse of rejection from the womb or illegitimacy which may be in my family back to 10 generations on both sides of any family.
9. I break all the curses of deformity, infirmity and sickness in my family back to 10 generations on both sides of my family, in the name of Jesus.
10. Let my God arise and put to flight every mind-controlling spirit, in the name of Jesus.

DESTINY MARCHING ORDERS

YOU MUST MOVE FROM BEING A COPY TO BEING AN ORIGINAL

Scientist have discovered that of over seven billion people on earth, no two finger prints are the same. This shows that every human being on earth is unique in every sense. Living as a photocopy of others around you is to diminish your status. God has not created you to copy what others are doing. You have unique attributes and special qualities that would make you stand out any day.

God has created you to take your place in the classroom of destiny and function like no other person. There is something in you that cannot be found in the life of any other human being on earth. God wants you to recognise your uniqueness and to live and function as an original. One of the ingredients of destiny is originality. The Bible says, "I am fearfully and wonderfully made."

When you copy others, you are guilty of the following offences:
1. Spiritual blindness.
2. Intellectual suicide.
3. Assault on the Almighty.
4. Limiting yourself.
5. Limiting God.
6. Destiny suicide.
7. You have chosen to become a dropout in the school of destiny.
8. You have chosen to become a failure in the race of life.

Copying others stems from the fact that you are grossly ignorant of God's purpose and plan for your life. The moment God opens your eyes to the fact that He has loaded you with uncommon spiritual wealth, you will no longer stoop low to the level of copying others. You must pray until you discover your originality.

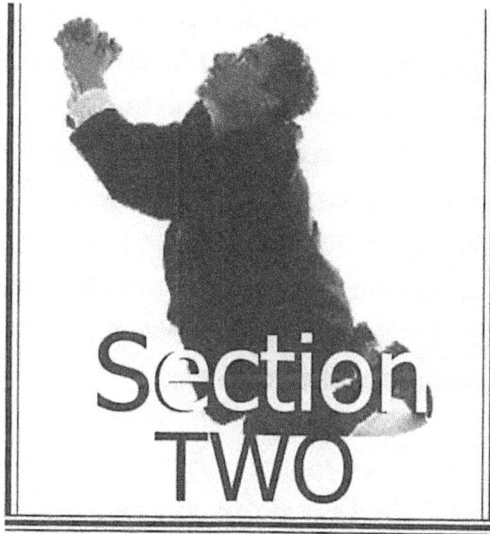

DESTINY CONFESSIONS

My life is a perfect demonstration of God's unique ability to make the destiny of man original in every sense. God is theAuthor and the Finisher of my faith. Jesus is my perfect example. He is my mentor and role model. I cannot bring myself to a level where I become only a copy of others. God has made me unique. I am an original. I am not a victim of the, "copy syndrome." I cannot bring myself low to the point of being a photocopy of others. My uniqueness, forbids that I imitate others sheepishly. I am original is every sense. My destiny is unique. My talent and gifts are original. I shall not run after shadows. I celebrate the virtues of God within me. I celebrate the deposits of grace upon my life. I am an original in every sense. God does not create mere copies. His endowments within me are too original to be toyed with. My talents are original. My qualities are real. My God-given goal cannot be compared with anyone else's. I am committed to the exploration of my hidden talents and gifts. I shall maximise my divine potentials. I shall continue to improve myself until the whole world beholds the glory and the beauty of God upon my life. I refuse to sweep my goodness under the carpet. I am bringing to the fore the exquisite qualities given to me. The whole world shall behold the original nature of the unique qualities invested in me.

Spirit of favour, counsel, might and power, come upon me, in the name of Jesus. I shall excel this day and nothing shall defile me. I shall possess the gates of my enemies. The Lord shall anoint me with the oil of gladness above my fellows. The fire of the enemy shall not burn me. My ears shall hear good news and I shall not hear the voice of the enemy. My future is secured in Christ, in the name of Jesus.

God has created me to do some definite services. He has committed into my hands some assignments which He has not committed to anybody else. He has not created me for nothing. There will be no poverty of body, soul and spirit in my life. The anointing of God upon my life gives me favour in the eyes of God and man all the days of my life. I shall not labour in vain. I shall walk this day in victory and liberty of the spirit.

I receive the mouth and the wisdom which my adversaries are not able to resist, in Jesus' name. I declare that Satan and his wicked spirits are under my feet, in the name of Jesus. I claim the victory of the Cross for my life today and everybody. In the name of Jesus. Every satanic foothold in my life, be dismantled by fire, in the name of Jesus.

Section
THREE

DESTINY SCRIPTURES

O LORD our Lord, how excellent is thy name in all the earth! who hast set thy glory above the heavens. Out of the mouth of babes and sucklings hast thou ordained strength because of thine enemies, that thou mightest still the enemy and the avenger. When I consider thy heavens, the work of thy fingers, the moon and the stars, which thou hast ordained; What is man, that thou art mindful of him? and the son of man, that thou visitest him? For thou hast made him a little lower than the angels, and hast crowned him with glory and honour. Thou madest him to have dominion over the works of thy hands; thou hast put all things under his feet: All sheep and oxen, yea, and the beasts of the field; The fowl of the air, and the fish of the sea, and whatsoever passeth through the paths of the seas. O LORD our Lord, how excellent is thy name in all the earth! Ps. 8:1-9.

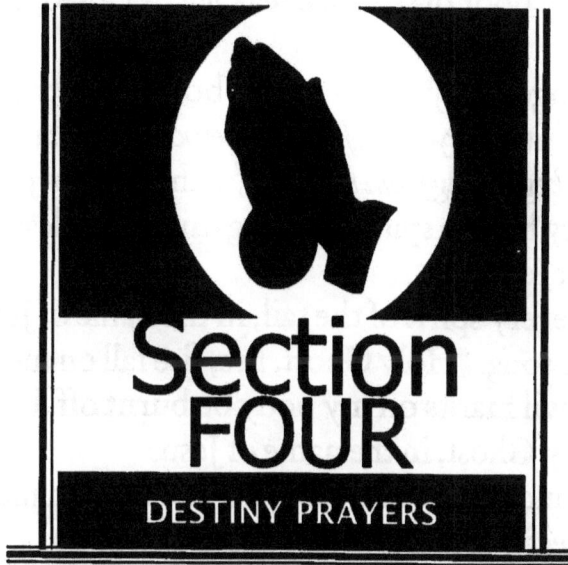

Section FOUR

DESTINY PRAYERS

Day 1

1. Thank God for the revelational power of the Holy Spirit.
2. Thank God for the purifying power of the Holy Ghost.
3. I cover myself with the blood of the Lord Jesus.
4. Father, let Your fire that burns away every deposit of the enemy fall upon me, in the name of Jesus.
5. Holy Ghost, incubate me, in the name of the Lord Jesus Christ.
6. I reject any stamp or seal placed upon me by ancestral spirits, in the name of Jesus.
7. I release myself from every negative anointing, in the name of Jesus.

8. Let every door of spiritual leakage be closed, in the name of Jesus.

9. I challenge every organ of my body with the fire of the Holy Spirit. (*Lay your right hand methodically on various parts of the body beginning from the head*), in the name of Jesus.

10. Let every human spirit attacking my spirit release me, in the name of Jesus.

11. I reject every spirit of the tail, in the name of Jesus.

12. Sing the song: "Holy Ghost, fire, fire fall on me."

13. Let all evil marks on my body be burnt off .by the fire of the Holy Ghost, in the name of Jesus.

14. Let the anointing of the Holy Ghost fall upon me and break every negative yoke, in the name of Jesus.

15. Let every garment of hindrance and dirtiness be dissolved by the fire of the Holy Ghost, in the name of Jesus.

16. I command all my chained blessings to be unchained, in the name of Jesus.

Day 2

1. Let all spiritual cages inhibiting my progress be roasted by the fire of the Holy Spirit, in Jesus' name.
2. Lord, give unto me the spirit of revelation and wisdom in the knowledge of you.
3. Lord, make your way plain before my face on this issue.
4. Lord, remove spiritual cataract from my eyes.
5. Lord, forgive me for every false motive or thought that has ever been formed in my heart since I was born.
6. Lord, forgive me for any lie that I have ever told against any person; system or organisation.
7. Lord, deliver me from the bondage and sin of spiritual laziness.
8. Lord, open my eyes to see all that I should see on this issue.
9. Lord, teach me deep and secret things.
10. Lord, reveal to me every secret behind any problem that I have.
11. Lord, bring to light everything planned against me in darkness.
12. Lord, ignite and revive my beneficial potentials.
13. Lord, give me divine wisdom to operate my life.
14. Lord, let every veil preventing me from having plain spiritual vision be removed.
15. Lord, give unto me the spirit of revelation and wisdom in the knowledge of you.
16. Lord, open up my spiritual understanding.

Day 3

1. Holy Spirit, reveal deep and secret things to me about...., in the name of Jesus.
2. I bind every demon that pollutes spiritual visions and dreams, in the name of Jesus.
3. Let every dirtiness blocking my communication pipe with the living God be washed clean by the blood of Jesus, in the name of Jesus. .
4. I receive power to operate with sharp spiritual eyes that cannot be deceived, in the name of Jesus.
5. Let the glory and the power of the Almighty God fall upon my life in a mighty way, in the name of Jesus.
6. I remove my name from those who grope and stumble in darkness, in the name of Jesus.
7. Divine revelations, spiritual visions, dreams and information will not become scarce commodities in my life, in the name of Jesus.
8. I drink to the full in the well of salvation and anointing, in the name of Jesus.

DESTINY MARCHING ORDERS

YOU MUST MOVE FROM INGRATITUDE TO THANKSGIVING

God is the author of destiny. What you have become and what you will ever be can be attributed to Him. To be a success in the school of destiny, you must shun ingratitude. When you appreciate what God Has done in your life you will inspire Him to do more. But when you are full of ingratitude, you will limit God. The journey of destiny cannot be undertaken through carnal strength. As far as destiny is concerned, it is by the Lords' mercies that we are not consumed. You must appreciate God's faithfulness, evince a grateful heart and manifest the fact that your heart is filled with appreciation and adoration for what the Lord Has done so far in your life.

The journey of destiny can be seen from two perspectives. You can decide to manifest disillusionment as a result of what you have not achieved. You can also decide to show gratitude and joy for what God Has done. As far as destiny is concerned, your attitude determines your altitude. Negative attitude can truncate the journey of destiny. A positive attitude will facilitate the journey of destiny.

When you take a look at a bottle that contains some liquid, what you see can be viewed along two lines. If the liquid in the bottle reaches half of the bottle, you can either say that bottle is half-empty or half-full. When you dwell on emptiness, you are manifesting ingratitude. When you dwell on fullness, you are manifesting a thankful spirit. Thanksgiving will take your destiny to greater heights. You must spend time saying thanksgiving prayer points, if you want your destiny to reach maximum point.

Section TWO

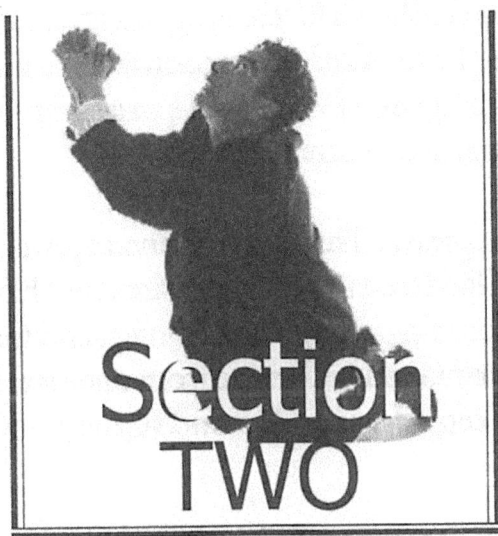

DESTINY CONFESSIONS

God is good to me. There is no denying the fact that He has been gracious unto me. I have counted my blessings and I am amazed at what God has done for me. I cannot be ungrateful for His past and present mercies. I cannot forget the fact that He has been good to my Israel. His presence has made a great difference is my life. His power has sustained me. His peace has calmed my anxious nerves. His blessings have made me rich. His grace has been lavished upon me. He has bombarded me with spiritual benefits. For all these I am filled with gratitude.

Nothing on earth can make me go back to ingratitude. I cannot murmur. I cannot complain. I refuse to focus my attention on sadness and sorrow. I cannot take the goodness of God for granted. My heart is filled with thanksgiving and praise. My lips shall sing of the Lord. With my mouth will I make known faithfulness to all generations. I will praise my God in the morning, at noon and at night.

I am addicted to praise. Thanksgiving and appreciation shall always go up to God from my life. I declare that I have become a specialist in according praise, thanksgiving and worship unto God. As I praise my God I will move from one level of grace to another. I will keep praising God and my joy will begin to overflow.

I am a saint. I belong to God. I am a king and a royal priest called to the service of God. Jesus bought me with His own precious and blameless blood and has translated my life from the kingdom of darkness into His kingdom of light, peace and abundant life.

I stand on the victory of Jesus over satan and over death and hell, for it is written that Jesus first of all descended into the lower parts of the earth and stripped the devil of his power and ascended on high leading captivity captive and gave gifts unto men. By this victory, let every gathering of the powers of darkness that is against my prayer life, my success and my breakthrough, be defeated by the blood of Jesus.

The day I wholeheartedly gave my life to Christ, I submitted myself to the authority of the God of hosts. Therefore, Satan,

20 Marching Orders to Fulfil Your Destiny

I have authority to resist you and your attacks against my sound relationship with my Maker, Jehovah God. Through my faith in Jesus Christ, I have become a seed of Abraham. The blessings of Abraham are mine.

The Scriptures say that I am blessed with faithful Abraham. I am a partaker of all God's heavenly blessings. It is written that God has blessed all His children with all spiritual blessings in the heavenly places. The Lord God is a Sun and Shield and I believe in Him because those who do not are already condemned. Therefore, I tear down in faith, every spiritual wall of partition between me and my divinely appointed helpers and benefactors.

Section
THREE

DESTINY SCRIPTURES

O LORD our Lord, how excellent is thy name in all the earth! who hast set thy glory above the heavens. Out of the mouth of babes and sucklings hast thou ordained strength because of thine enemies, that thou mightest still the enemy and the avenger. When I consider thy heavens, the work of thy fingers, the moon and the stars, which thou hast ordained; What is man, that thou art mindful of him? and the son of man, that thou visitest him? For thou hast made him a little lower than the angels, and hast crowned him with glory and honour. Thou madest him to have dominion over the works of thy hands; thou hast put all things under his feet: All sheep and oxen, yea, and the beasts of the field; The fowl of the air, and the fish of the sea, and whatsoever passeth through the paths of the seas. O LORD our Lord, how excellent is thy name in all the earth! Ps. 8:1-9.

Praise ye the LORD. Praise ye the LORD from the heavens: praise him in the heights. Praise ye him, all his angels: praise ye him, all his hosts. Praise ye him, sun and moon: praise him, all ye stars of light. Praise him, ye heavens of heavens, and ye waters that be above the heavens. Let them praise the name of the LORD: for he commanded, and they were created. He hath also stablished them for ever and ever: he hath made a decree which shall not pass. Praise the LORD from the earth, ye dragons, and all deeps: Fire, and hail; snow, and vapour; stormy wind fulfilling his word: Mountains, and all hills; fruitful trees, and all cedars: Beasts, and all cattle; creeping things, and flying fowl: Kings of the earth, and all people; princes, and all judges of the earth: Both young men, and maidens; old men, and children: Let them praise the name of the LORD: for his name alone is excellent; his glory is above the earth and heaven. He also exalteth the horn of his people, the praise of all his saints; even of the children of Israel, a people near unto him. Praise ye the LORD. Ps. 148:1-14.

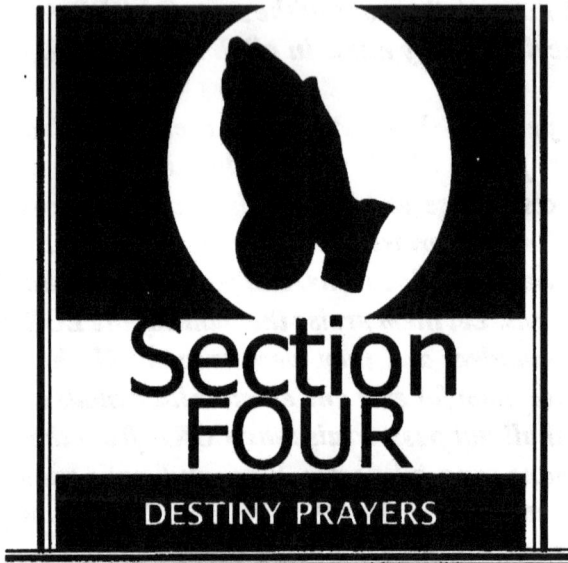

Section FOUR

DESTINY PRAYERS

Day 1

1. I send back to the sender, every arrow of spiritual deposit and advance payment against my handiwork, in the name of Jesus.
2. You my handiwork, receive divine profit, in the name of Jesus.
3. I cover my handiwork with the fire of God, in the name of Jesus.
4. I cover my handiwork with hot coals of fire untouchable by evil forces, in the name of Jesus.
5. Lord, put to shame every evil force that is against my handiwork.
6. My handiwork, receive the touch of the Lord, in Jesus' name.

7. Every tree of profitless handiwork, be uprooted, in Jesus' name.
8. Profitless hard-work, pack your load and go out of my life, in the name of Jesus.
9. I will not carry any evil load forward in my life, in Jesus' name.
10. Lord, drain out satanic deposits from my business and handiwork.
11. Let all the strange hands and legs walk out of my business and handiwork, in the name of Jesus.
12. Let the' spirit of favour fall upon me now, in the name of Jesus.
13. Lord, enlarge my coast.
14. 1 rebuke every devourer in my handiwork, in the name of Jesus.
15. Lord, cause ministering angels to bring in customers and money into my business.
16. I bind every spirit of error, in the name of Jesus.
17. Let every trouble emanating from envious business partners be rendered null and void, in the name of Jesus.
18. Lord, surprise me with abundance in every area of my life.

Day 2

1. Let all my mistakes be converted to miracles and testimonies, in the name of Jesus.
2. I command all those who vowed to hinder my prosperity to somersault, become naked and confess to death, in Jesus' name.
3. I command all my buried blessings to be exhumed, in Jesus' name.
4. Father Lord, use both white and black men to bless me, in the name of Jesus.
5. I command all my pounds and dollars' miracles, to locate me, in the name of Jesus.
6. All my blessings attached to my place of birth, be released, in the name. of Jesus.
7. Father Lord, use all the people in my environment to bless me and let the anointing of prosperity fall on me, in the name of Jesus.
8. Lord, by the power of the blood, remove from my life any hindrance of the enemy.
9. Lord, drive away all darkness in every area of my life.
10. Lord, shield me from all forms of deception.
11. Lord, illuminate Your truth to my understanding.
12. Lord, let me see You clearly with the eyes of my heart.
13. Lord, take away from me all powers that do not originate from You.

14. I separate myself from Satan and his kingdom, in Jesus' name.
15. I renounce the kingdom of darkness and embrace the kingdom of Jesus Christ, in the name of Jesus.
16. Lord Jesus, deliver me from evil.

Day 3

1. I apply the blood of Jesus Christ to break all evil curses upon my life, in the name of Jesus.
2. I shall be anointed with fresh oil from' heaven, in Jesus' name.
3. Lord, reveal to me strongholds that hinder revival in my life, in the name of Jesus.
4. Lord Jesus, let a deep work begin in my heart.
5. I kill all strange animals sent against me with the sword of the Lord, in the name of Jesus.
6. I divorce every satanic husband, in the name of Jesus.
7. Let the fire of God be released on every demonic child in my life, in the name of Jesus.
8. Let all evil spiritual homes be burnt down, in the name of Jesus.
9. I reject the spirit of slavery and hardship in every area of my life, in the name of Jesus.
10. Let the spirit of delay and hindrance be cast out of my life, in the name of Jesus.
11. I dissolve every anti-breakthrough strategy, in Jesus' name
12. Let the hands of evil refuse to perform their enterprise in any area of my life, in the name of Jesus.
13. I decree that there shall not be compromise and dialogue between me and my enemies, in the name of Jesus.
14. I pull down all strongholds of evil over my life and the live

of any member of my family, in the name of Jesus.

15. Lord, close the gap between where I am and where You want me to be.

16. Let all demonic jailers be roasted, in the name of Jesus.

17. Thank the Lord for answered prayers.

Day 4

1. Thank the Lord from the bottom of your heart for what He will use this prayer programme to do in your life.
2. I reject every backward journey, in the name of Jesus.
3. Let every agent of shame working against me be paralysed, in the name of Jesus.
4. I paralyse the activities of household wickedness over my life, in the name of Jesus.
5. I quench every strange fire emanating from evil tongues against me, in the name of Jesus.
6. Lord, give me the confronting authority to achieve effortless results.
7. Lord, fill me with wisdom like an angel.
8. I break every curse of unfruitfulness placed upon my life, in the name of Jesus.
9. I break every curse of untimely death, in the name of Jesus.
10. Lord, fortify me with Your power.
11. Let the counter-movement of the Holy Spirit frustrate every evil device against me, in the name of Jesus.
12. Father Lord, give me the tongue of the learned.
13. Lord, make my voice the voice of peace, deliverance, power and solution.
14. Every power assigned to use my family/job, etc. to torment me, be paralysed, in the name of Jesus.
15. Lord Jesus, give me an excellent spirit.
16. Thank God for answered prayers.

DESTINY MARCHING ORDERS

YOU MUST MOVE FROM PROCRASTINATION TO PROGRESS

Destiny is a product of action. Actions lead to progress. Being passive leads to failure. If you keep putting till tomorrow what you can do and achieve today, your destiny would remain in doldrums. Procrastination, they say, is the thief of time. It will not only steal your time but also your destiny. Many destinies are victims of thefts perpetrated by procrastination.

It is an enemy of progress. The devil knows that if you take proper actions you will experience destiny fulfillment. Hence, he tries to discourage you from taking any action whatsoever. When he discovers that you are bent on taking actions, he will tell you to hold on a little or delay until a more 'convenient' time. When you buy his procrastination, you will keep on delaying. Eventually you would make no progress.

There is a king in the Bible who had the opportunity of taking a life changing-decision, but he gave in to procrastination.

Acts 26:24-28:

> *And as he thus spake for himself, Festus said with a loud voice, Paul, thou art beside thyself; much learning doth make thee mad. But he said, I am not mad, most noble Festus; but speak forth the words of truth and soberness. For the king knoweth of these things, before whom also I speak freely: Ofor I am persuaded that none of these things are hidden from him; for this thing was not done in a corner. King Agrippa, believest thou the prophets? I know that thou believest. Then Agrippa said unto Paul, Almost thou persuadest me to be a Christian.*

Agrippa was almost persuaded and an almost saved soul, but he was not fully persuaded. He must have thought of a more convenient time when he would be fully persuaded. To take a better decision. By postponing his moment of decision he lost a golden chance. It is unfortunate today, that the graveyard has become the richest place in the universe. It has become a home to books that were never written, songs that were never sung, houses that were never built and several projects that were never completed. If you have ever procrastinated, I put it to you that you have lots of uncompleted projects. You would have gone further and further, if not for the destiny thief called procrastination. The matching orders here, is that procrastination must die and progress must begin by fire.

Section
THREE

DESTINY SCRIPTURES

Give not sleep to thine eyes, nor slumber to thine eyelids. Deliver thyself as a roe from the hand of the hunter, and as a bird from the hand of the fowler. Go to the ant, thou sluggard; consider her ways, and be wise: Which having no guide, overseer, or ruler, Provideth her meat in the summer, and gathereth her food in the harvest. How long wilt thou sleep, O sluggard? when wilt thou arise out of thy sleep? Yet a little sleep, a little slumber, a little folding of the hands to sleep: So shall thy poverty come as one that travelleth, and thy want as an armed man. Prov 6:4-11.

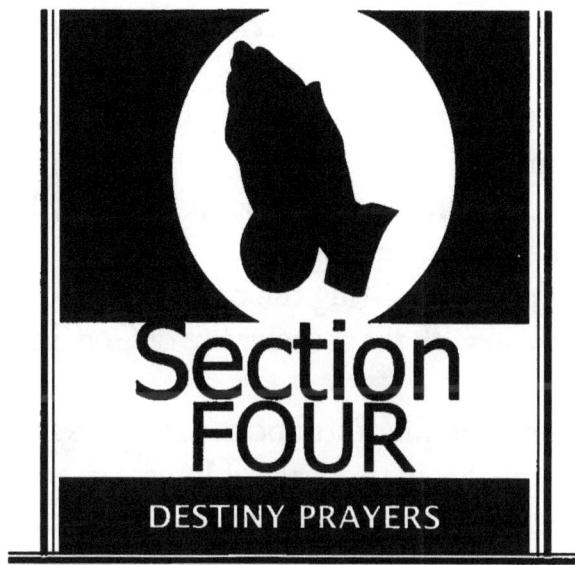

Day 1

1. Every household enemy resisting my breakthroughs, fall down and die, in the name of Jesus.
2. Every unfriendly friend delegated against my blessing, scatter, in the name of Jesus.
3. Every spirit of disobedience and rebellion in my life, die, in the name of Jesus.
4. Every demon propagating satanic covenants in my life, fall down and die, in the name of Jesus.
5. Any organ in my body presently on any evil altar, be roasted; in the name of Jesus.
6. By the stripes of Jesus I curse the roots of every sickness in my life, in the name of Jesus.

7.   I destroy any anchor of any bondage in my life, in the name of Jesus.

8.   Every spirit of hardship in my life, loose your hold, in the name of Jesus.

9.   Every problem that defies solution in my life, blood of Jesus destroy it, in the name of Jesus.

10. Every power resisting the power of God in my life, I attack you with the thunder fire of God, in the name of Jesus.

11. Every mountain of stubborn problems in my life, fall down and die, in the name of Jesus.

12. Every invisible hand working evil in my life, wither, in the name of Jesus.

13. Every demon of frustration in my life, die, in the name of Jesus.

14. I reject every spirit of rejection and cancel its operations in my life, in the name of Jesus.

15. I reject and cast out of my life every deeply-rooted failure, in the name of Jesus

16. Every spirit of abject poverty in my family line, my life is not your candidate, die, in the name of Jesus.

17. Holy Ghost fire, burn every garment of poverty in my life, in the name of Jesus.

Day 2

1. Every spirit of blindness in my life, die, in the name of Jesus.
2. Every spirit of poverty in my foundation, die, in the name of Jesus.
3. Every problem planned for my future, you shall not see the daylight, in the name of Jesus.
4. Every warfare against my breakthroughs in the heavenlies, scatter, in the name of Jesus.
5. Let every cycle of problems in my life die, in the name of Jesus.
6. By the blood of Jesus, I make my breakthroughs untouchable for any evil power, in the name of Jesus.
7. You powers working against my treasures, fall down and die, in the name of Jesus.
8. Thank God for answers to your prayers.
9. Thank God for making provision for deliverance from any form of bondage.
10. Confess your sins and those of your ancestors, especially those linked to evil powers.
11. I cover myself with the blood of Jesus.
12. I release myself from any inherited bondage, in Jesus' name.
13. Lord, send Your axe of fire to the foundation of my life and destroy every evil plantation.
14. Let the blood of Jesus flush out from my system every

inherited satanic deposit, in the name of Jesus.

15. I release myself from the grip of any problem transferred into my life from the womb, in the name of Jesus

Day 3

1. You evil foundational plantation, come out of my life with all your roots, in the name of Jesus.
2. I break and loose myself from every demonic bewitchment, in the name of Jesus.
3. I release myself from every evil domination and control, in the name of Jesus.
4. Let the blood of Jesus be transfused into my blood vessel.
5. Let every gate opened to the enemy by my foundation be closed for ever with the blood of Jesus.
6. Lord Jesus, walk back into every second of my life and deliver me where I need deliverance, heal me where I need healing, transform me where I need transformation.
7. Thou power of God, penetrate my spirit, soul and body, in .the name of Jesus.
8. Association of demons gathered against my progress, be roasted by the thunder fire of God, in the name of Jesus.
9. Blood of Jesus, redeem me, in the name of Jesus.
10. Every satanic decision taken against my progress, be nullified, in the name of Jesus.
11. Every evil deposit in my spirit, soul and body, be flushed out by the blood of Jesus, in the name of Jesus.
12. Oh Lord my God, promote me in the spiritual and in the physical, in the name of Jesus.
13. Every stranger in my body (ministry, life and calling), jump out, in the name of Jesus.

14. Any satanic arrow fired at me, go back, locate and destroy your sender, in the name of Jesus.

15. Holy Ghost, arise and destroy the habitation and works of the wicked.

DESTINY MARCHING ORDERS

YOU MUST MOVE FROM EVIL HESITATION TO OBEDIENCE

Obedience has become a rare commodity. Many hesitate and drag their feet when it comes to the issue of obedience. God treasures obedience while the devil loves disobedience and rebellion.

God is ever busy speaking to His children. But when we hesitate to listen to Him, the journey of destiny is slowed down. Disobedience can be so strong as to put a full stop to the journey of destiny. The Bible tells us that "Obedience is better than sacrifice." As far as Heaven is concerned 99 per cent obedience is not good enough. God is asking for 100 per cent obedience. There is no way you can fulfill your destiny if you default in the area of obedience.

God knows the end from the beginning. He knows what is required to make your destiny a huge success. When He gives you a divine instruction, He expects prompt, total and unquestionable obedience. When He sends you on an assignment He expects you to rise up instantly.

When we do the will of God, He abides with us. Obedience will make you a favorite of the Almighty. When you keep obeying Him, you become an apple of His eyes. But disobedience will keep you at arms length.

You must move as fast as you can out of the valley of disobedience or crafty hesitation. The only thing you can do to gladden the heart of God is to obey Him in all ramifications.

Obedience will draw commitment from the Almighty. As you obey Him, He will take care of all that concern you. The challenge of the hour today is to surrender yourself on the altar of obedience.

Romans 12:1-2 says:

> *I beseech you therefore, brethren, by the mercies of God, that ye present your bodies a living sacrifice, holy, acceptable unto God, which is your reasonable service. And be not conformed to this world: but be ye transformed by the renewing of your mind, that ye may*

prove what is that good, and acceptable, and perfect, will of God.

God is calling you to obedience today. As you build your destiny on the platform of obedience through the prayer session below, you will experience a great lift.

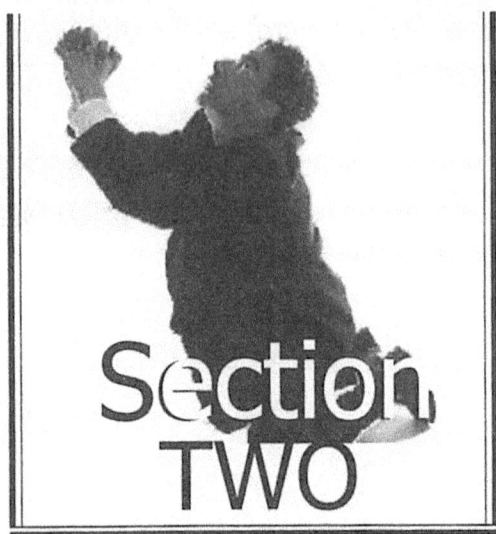

Section TWO

DESTINY CONFESSIONS

I am created in the image and the likeness of God. I have been recreated unto glory after the image of the Lord Jesus Christ. By the finished work of Calvary, I have been set free from negative encumbrances. I am free from evil hesitation. I am free from every act of dragging my feet, sponsored by enemies of my progress. I refuse to be dragged back by anti-progress powers.

I soar into great height, with the speed of the eagle. I move higher and higher into the realm of obedience. I command every cell in my body to become captive of divine obedience. I have moved from the realm of hesitation and reluctance to the realm of prompt and unquestioning obedience.

I shall obey God at all times. The spirit of obedience has fallen upon me. The power of obedience has entered my bones. When God speaks I will obey instantly. The commandments of God have become my pleasure. I am a captive of the spirit of obedience. My spirit, soul and body are sold out to the Almighty. I am an embodiment of obedience, a specimen of a life that is lived to the glory of God. It is no longer I who lives, but Christ who lives in me.

I shall obey promptly. I shall obey perfectly. I shall obey from the depth of my heart. My destiny has put on the garment of obedience. I am a student in the school of Christ. Therefore, I have learnt obedience. No more evil hesitation!

I am not what the world thinks or say I am. I am not what the devil or the kingdom of darkness says I am, or imagines or has designed me to be. I am not the picture of what my idolatrous forefathers wished I should be. I am not what the unregenerate mind thinks I should be. I am not what my village wickedness wants me to be. I am not a picture of what the national economy and institutionalised wickedness have restricted many people to be. I am not what I think I am. I am what the word of God says I am. I am an express image of Jehovah God on earth.

I am regenerated by the blood of Jesus. I am ransomed from the powers of death and hell. I am blood washed. I am redeemed. I am justified by Christ. I am made to be the righteousness of God through Christ. I am a believer of the word of Truth. I am born again; I am heaven-bound; my citizenship is in heaven. I am seated with Christ in the heavenly places, far above principalities, powers and dominions. I am a priest and a king ordained by Christ to rule here on earth. I am the fear and the dread of God against the kingdom of darkness. I am a dwelling place of the Holy Spirit of God. I am built up together and attached to other children of God into a holy habitation of God. No power contrary to God's can change that. Amen.

The word of God says that I am a royal priesthood, I am a holy nation; I am a chosen generation and a peculiar person, I am special in the sight of God. The Bible says, because I believe and have received Jesus Christ, power has been given to me to become the son of God. I am empowered to trample upon serpents and scorpions and over all the power of the enemy. I am empowered to use the name of Jesus to cast out demons and heal the sick. I am empowered to bind, to loose and to decree things. The Bible says that wherever my voice is heard no one can ask me why. I do these things for my voice is the voice of the king, full of authority.

Section
THREE

DESTINY SCRIPTURES

My son, forget not my law; but let thine heart keep my commandments: For length of days, and long life, and peace, shall they add to thee. Let not mercy and truth forsake thee: bind them about thy neck; write them upon the table of thine heart: So shalt thou find favour and good understanding in the sight of God and man. Trust in the LORD with all thine heart; and lean not unto thine own understanding. In all thy ways acknowledge him, and he shall direct thy paths. Prov 3:1-6.

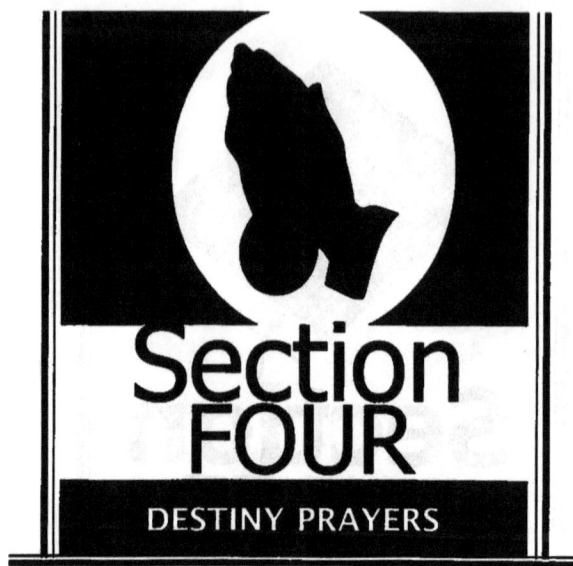

Section FOUR

DESTINY PRAYERS

Day 1

1. Praise the Lord for the power in His name at which every knee must bow.
2. Every ancestral covenant affecting my life, break and loose your hold, in the name of Jesus
3. Every inherited family covenant affecting my life, break and loose your hold, in the name of Jesus.
4. Every inherited covenant affecting my life, break and release me, in the name of Jesus.
5. Any evil covenant prospering in my family, be broken by the blood of Jesus.
6. Every soul-tie and covenant between me and ancestral spirits, break and release me, in the name of Jesus

7. Every soul-tie and covenant with any dead relation, break now and release me, in the name of Jesus.

8. Every soul-tie and covenant with family gods, shrines and spirits, break and release me, in the name of Jesus. .

9. Every soul-tie and covenant between me and my parents, break and release me, in the name of Jesus.

10. Every soul-tie between me and my grandparents, break and release me, in the name of Jesus.

11. Every soul-tie covenant between me and former boyfriends or girlfriends, break and loose your hold, in the name of Jesus.

12. Every soul-tie covenant between me and any spirit husband or wife, break and loose your hold, in the name of Jesus.

13. Every soul-tie covenant between me and demonic ministers, break and loose your hold, in the name of Jesus.

14. Every soul-tie covenant between me and my former house, office or school, break and loose your hold, in the name of Jesus.

15. Every soul-tie covenant between me and water spirits, break and loose your hold, in the name of Jesus.

16. Every soul-tie covenant between me and serpentine spirits, break and loose your hold, in the name of Jesus. .

17. Any covenant empowering my household enemies, break and loose your hold, in the name of Jesus.

18. Every soul-tie covenant between me and occult relations, break and loose your hold, in the name of Jesus.

19. Every soul-tie covenant between me and any dead relation, break and loose your hold, in the name of Jesus.

20. Any evil covenant strengthening the foundation of any bondage, be broken, in the name of Jesus.
21. Every soul-tie covenant between me and familiar spirit, break and loose your hold, in the name of Jesus.
22. Every soul-tie covenant between me and spiritual night caterers, break and loose your hold, in the name of Jesus.
23. Every soul-tie covenant between me and any territorial spirit, break and loose your hold, in the name of Jesus.

Day 2

1. Every demonic mark and incision on my body, be washed off by the blood of Jesus.
2. I nullify every covenant, oath and promise made in occult houses and shrines, in the name of Jesus.
3. Blood of Jesus, close every doorway of demonic invasion into my life, in the name of Jesus.
4. Blood of Jesus, purge my soul, spirit and body of every occultic property, in the name of Jesus.
5. I loose my destiny from every grip of occult demons, in the name of Jesus.
6. Every spirit of the bondwoman working in my life, be cast out by fire, in the name of Jesus.
7. Every evil link and contact with demons over the years, break now, in the name of Jesus
8. Every occultic agreement and covenant made with powers of darkness, break by the blood of Jesus.
9. Every evil knowledge I acquired from occult associations, be flushed out of my life, by the blood of Jesus.
10. I declare myself free from every occultic entanglement, in the name of Jesus.

Day 3

1. Lord, give me the spirit of obedience.
2. Let all the powers that shake off God's blessings in my life, be removed and be destroyed, in the name of Jesus.
3. I place myself now, under the cross of Jesus.
4. I cover myself, with the precious blood of Jesus.
5. I surround myself, with the light of Christ.
6. The devil, will not interfere with the Lord's work in my life, in the name of Jesus.
7. I put on God's armour, to resist the devil's tactics, in Jesus' name.
8. Lord, reveal to me, any way that satan has a hold on my life.
9. I claim back, any territory of my life handed over to satan, in the name of Jesus.
10. I bind, all forces of evil in the air, fire, water and ground being set in motion against my life, in the name of Jesus.
11. I forbid any spirit from any source from harming me in any way, in the name of Jesus.
12. I reject every spirit of seduction, in the name of Jesus.
13. I refuse to let sin have dominion over me, in the name of Jesus.
14. I reject every satanic promise on any department of my life, in the name of Jesus.
15. Let the powers setting themselves up in opposition to me be paralysed, in the name of Jesus.

16. I cancel the effect of all former satanic benefits in my life, in the name of Jesus.
17. I bind you spirit of anger in my life, in the name of Jesus.
18. Lord, fill me with strength to replace weakness.
19. Let all spiritual contamination be washed away by the blood of Jesus.
20. Let the cleansing and healing waters of the Lord flow into my life now, in the name of Jesus.
21. Father, I surrender to you today, with all my heart and soul, in the name of Jesus.
22. Lord, come into my home in a deeper way.
23. I say yes to you today, O Lord.
24. I open all the secret places of my heart to you. Come in, Lord Jesus.
25. I surrender, every department of my life to you, O Lord, in the name of Jesus.
26. I surrender my past, present and future to you, O Lord.
27. Come, Holy Spirit and baptise me with the fire of Your love, in the name of Jesus.

DESTINY MARCHING ORDERS

YOU MUST MOVE FROM BEING FULL OF PRIDE TO BEING FULL OF GOD

This is one destiny marching order you must take seriously if you want to experience destiny fulfilment. The Bible makes it very clear that pride is the fore-runner of failure. When you are full of pride you will become a candidate of failure in the school of destiny. Most people who are casualties in the field of destiny came to that by allowing the cancer of pride to get into their destiny.

Pride can shut the door of the warehouse of destiny. It can bar you from gaining entrance into the house of destiny. It can prolong your journey and truncate your joys as far as your destiny is concerned. It can turn you into a leper who is disqualified from the race of destiny. It can empty your destiny of every good thing that is required to make it stand. It will puncture the balloon of your destiny. It will disqualify you from receiving any award during the celebration of destiny.

Pride can pull you down from great heights. It will render your destiny unfit to undertake the journey of life. It will make you deaf, dumb and blind. It will drag you to hell like an evil magnet. It will make you an enemy of your destiny and a friend of your destroyers. When you are full of self, you will be emptied of all the ingredients needed to fulfil your destiny.

What you need more than any other thing is the fullness of God. God will do nothing concerning your destiny until you have stripped your heart naked and ask Him to purge you and fill you with His glory.

The glory of God and pride will never mix. Your destiny will manifest powerfully the moment you move from being filled with pride to being filled with the fullness of God. The fullness of God will make great difference in your destiny. Pride is an evidence that the flesh is in control. The flesh is too heavy a burden to carry to the land of destiny. When you are filled with God, your life will be light and your journey to the land of destiny fulfilment will become a pleasurable ride. God's grace will manifest powerfully.

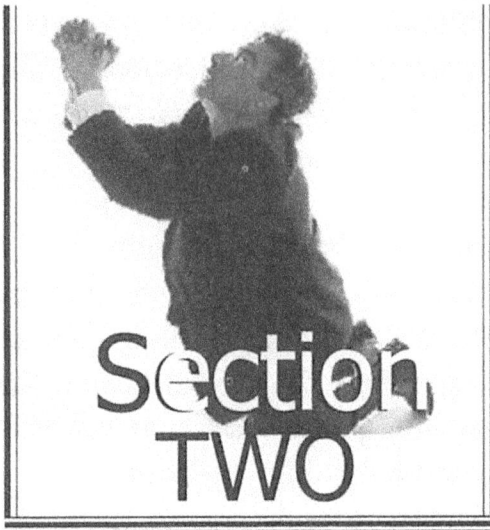

DESTINY CONFESSIONS

I am a pilgrim to Calvary. The cross has captured my heart, transformed my character and changed my values. I am a new creature in Christ. I am a walking symbol of brokenness, an example of Christ's likeness and an apostle that portrays the beauty of Jesus. Pride has died, lust has been slain, carnality has been buried and the flesh has received mortal wounds. My life is no longer mine. My heart is no longer under my control. It has become an altar of holiness. The Holy Spirit is at the driver's seat. It is now none of self and all of Christ. All traces of pride are gone. There is no more boasting and bragging.

Since I have nothing that I did not receive from God, I hereby repudiate all claims to personal achievement. In the past I allowed pride to capture me; now, I am no longer a candidate in the school of pride. In the past I was full of pride, now I am full of God. I set my heart on the task of exploring the fullness of God.

God is my preoccupation, He is my everything. He is my all. The fullness of God is my goal. I have decided to go higher and deeper with God. I shall allow God to fully manifest Himself in me. The fullest of God's character shall be visible in me. The heights of God shall be made manifest in me. I shall not make the valley of pride my place of abode. I am going higher with God.

I am no longer going to be full of myself. I shall overflow with grace, power, holiness, brokenness and godly character. My God shall take me higher. He shall empty me of self and vaulting pride and ambition. I am no longer proud of what I have achieved, what I possess and what I have become; God is now my passion. I want God and nothing else.

I put on the whole armour of God that I may be able to stand against the wiles of the devil. For I wrestle not against flesh and blood, but against principalities, against powers, against rulers of the darkness of this world, against spiritual wickedness in high places. I stand therefore, having my loins girded with truth, and having on the breastplate of righteousness; and my feet shod with the preparation of the gospel of peace. Above all, I take the shield of faith to quench all the fiery darts of the wicked one. And I take the helmet of salvation and the sword of the spirit which is the word of God, and the glory of the Lord is my reward.

I shall not war after the flesh, for the weapons of my warfare are not carnal, but mighty through God. No weapon that is formed against me shall prosper, and every tongue that shall rise against me in judgment shall be condemned.

Section
THREE
DESTINY SCRIPTURES

The preparations of the heart in man, and the answer of the tongue, is from the LORD. All the ways of a man are clean in his own eyes; but the LORD weigheth the spirits. Commit thy works unto the LORD, and thy thoughts shall be established. The LORD hath made all things for himself: yea, even the wicked for the day of evil. Every one that is proud in heart is an abomination to the LORD: though hand join in hand, he shall not be unpunished. By mercy and truth iniquity is purged: and by the fear of the LORD men depart from evil. When a man's ways please the LORD, he maketh even his enemies to be at peace with him. Prov. 16:1-7.

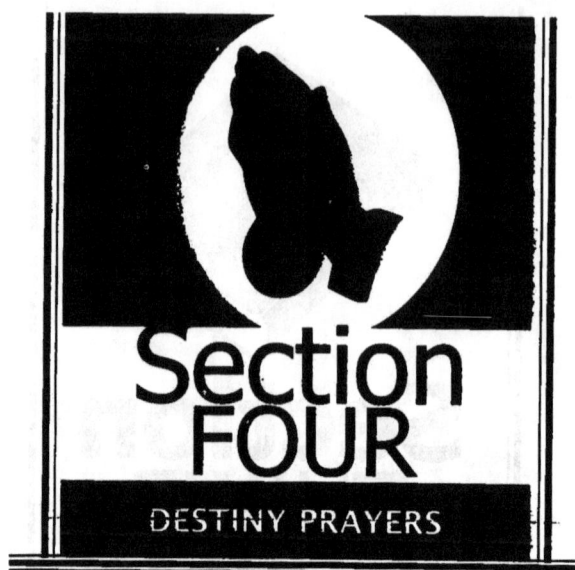

Section FOUR

DESTINY PRAYERS

Day 1

1. Lord, begin to baptise every area of my life with your dumbfounding miracles.
2. I nullify every evil effect of fear in my life, in the name of Jesus.
3. Holy Spirit, melt me, mould me, fill me and use me, in Jesus' name.
4. Holy Spirit, expand my capacity, in the name of Jesus.
5. Holy Spirit, work in me in a powerful way, in the name of Jesus.
6. Lord, let your purpose for my life be fulfilled.
7. Electric love of the Lord, flow into my being, in Jesus' name.
8. Lord, wash and cleanse me from past wounds and scars.

9. Lord, bring light into the shadows of my life.
10. Lord, bring light into all the workrooms in my soul.
11. Lord, uproot the root cause of any chronic failure in my life, in the name of Jesus.
12. Let all good things buried come alive, in the name of Jesus.
13. I reject every evil manipulation, in the name of Jesus.
14. I reject every deceptive family control, in the name of Jesus.
15. Let the curse of impossibility issued against me bounce back on the enemy, in the name of Jesus.
16. Let the agents of impossibility working against my desired miracles be completely paralysed, in the name of Jesus.
17. Let the plantations of impossibility in any department of my life receive fire and be roasted, in the name of Jesus.
18. I refuse to be diverted from the path of my blessings, in the name of Jesus.
19. Let every satanic angel deflecting blessings on my way stumble and fall, in the name of Jesus.
20. I command the powers drinking the milk of my life to begin to vomit it now, in the name of Jesus.

Day 2

1. Let every satan-inspired prayers against my life be reversed and turn to blessings, in the name of Jesus.
2. Let satanic access to my life be withdrawn completely, in the name of Jesus.
3. I curse every satanic mountain roblem in my life, in Jesus' name.
4. Let every fake friend in the camp of my life be exposed and disgraced, in the name of Jesus.
5. Let every evil collaborator in disguise be exposed and disgraced, in the name of Jesus.
6. Let all spiritual vultures wishing for my spiritual death be paralysed, in the name of Jesus.
7. Let no evil family river touch any area of my life, in Jesus' name.
8. Holy Spirit, help me to discover my very self, in Jesus' name.
9. I release my hand from every bewitchment, in the name of Jesus.
10. I forbid regrouping and reinforcement of any evil against my life, in the name of Jesus.
11. Let every vow of the enemy against my life be totally nullified, in the name of Jesus.
12. Lord, reverse all curses issued against me to good.
13. Let every satanic decision and judgment against my life become null and void, in the name of Jesus.

Day 3

1. Every evil device against me, be disappointed, in the name of Jesus.
2. Let the mighty healing power of God overshadow me now, in the name of Jesus.
3. I bind every spirit working against answers to my prayers, in the name of Jesus
4. I disarm any power that has made a covenant with the ground, water and wind against me, in the name of Jesus.
5. Lord, make my life invisible to demonic observers.
6. I bind all remote control spirits fashioned against me, in the name of Jesus.
7. I withdraw all the bullets and ammunition made available to the enemy, in the name of Jesus.
8. I revoke any conscious or unconscious covenant with the spirit of death, in the name of Jesus
9. Lord, I submit my tongue to you, take absolute control of it.
10. Let the heavenly Surgeon come down and perform surgical operations where necessary in my life, in the name of Jesus.
11. I refuse to be spiritually amputated, in the name of Jesus
12. I refuse to wage war against myself, in the name of Jesus.
13. Lord, wake me up from any form of spiritual sleep.
14. All evil seeds planted by fear into my life, be uprooted by the axes of God, in the name of Jesus.
15. Let your kingdom be established in every area of my life, O Lord.

DESTINY MARCHING ORDERS

YOU MUST MOVE FROM KEEPING TO GIVING

You must be a giver, not a keeper. If you have chosen to thread the pathway of an outstanding destiny, you must excel in the area of giving. Giving will make you stand out. You will remain a beggar, if you choose to keep what you have. Heaven has a special place for givers.

Keep what you have and you will become poorer. You can give your way to the land of prosperity. Keepers loose, givers get. The Bible tells us that when you give it shall be given unto you.

Luke 6:38 says:

Give, and it shall be given unto you; good measure, pressed down, and shaken together, and running over, shall men give into your bosom. For with the same measure that ye mete withal it shall be measured to you again.

The following facts emerge from the above passage:
1. Keep, and it shall be taken away from you.
2. Keep, and you shall lose what you tried to keep.
3. Give, and Heaven shall give unto you.
4. Heaven shall measure unto you a good measure.
5. It shall be pressed down to give room for more blessings.
6. It shall be shaken together to allow you to accommodate more benefits.
7. It shall be running over in order to allow you enjoy overflowing blessings.
8. Heaven has a measuring instrument to ensure that you are given the same measure which you give to others.
9. When you give unto men, men shall also give unto you

From the foregoing, it is crystal clear that your destiny rises or falls on your giving. Great givers stand to benefit from great prosperity. If you specialise in keeping or hoarding what you have, you will end up building a platform for poverty. If you want your destiny to be characterised by prosperity and wealth, begin to give today.

DESTINY CONFESSIONS

I am moving from keeping to giving. I have discovered that keepers lose and givers get. I refuse to be tight-fisted. I have taken up the character of God who gives and gives again. I am a giver not a selfish keeper. I received the spirit of giving. I shall give to God. I shall give to God's house. I shall give to the needy. As I give, I shall get. The spirit of generosity has fallen upon me. I am an incurable giver. I am committed to God's kingdom.

Selfishness has jumped out of my life. Since I cannot really keep what I posses, I have decided to give it over to God, who is the perfect keeper. I shall give unto God in tithes and offerings. I shall give unto Him, my first fruit offerings. I shall be involved in Church projects. I shall be a blessing to the needy.

I know that God will supply my need according to His riches in glory by Christ Jesus, since I have decided to be a treasurer of the Almighty. Whatever God blesses me with, shall be channeled towards meeting the needs of God's kingdom. I have decided to be in the forefront of giving. My destiny is tied to giving. I shall give and give to the glory of God.

Jesus, forgive my words of doubt an negativity. I loose all the wrong attitude and patterns of thinking I have about money, and I bind myself to God's truth. O Lord, renew my mind and attitude about Your provision and my real needs.

Your word says that if I sow sparingly I will reap sparingly. Help me to see if I am holding back what I need to share. Let me become a channel of Your deliverance. You are able and willing to make all grace come toward me, not so that I can indulge myself but so that I will have more than enough in all things and I can give, and help every good work.

Section THREE

DESTINY SCRIPTURES

Give, and it shall be given unto you; good measure, pressed down, and shaken together, and running over, shall men give into your bosom. For with the same measure that ye mete withal it shall be measured to you again. Luke 6:38.

He that hath pity upon the poor lendeth unto the LORD; and that which he hath given will he pay him again. Prov 19:17.

Will a man rob God? Yet ye have robbed me. But ye say, Wherein have we robbed thee? In tithes and offerings. Ye are cursed with a curse: for ye have robbed me, even this whole nation. Bring ye all the tithes into the storehouse, that there may be meat in mine house, and prove me now herewith, saith the LORD of hosts, if I will not open you the windows of heaven, and pour you out a blessing, that there shall not be room enough to receive it. And I will rebuke the devourer for your sakes, and he shall not destroy the fruits of your ground; neither shall your vine cast her fruit before the time in the field, saith the LORD of hosts. And all nations shall call you blessed: for ye shall be a delightsome land, saith the LORD of hosts. Mal 3:8-12.

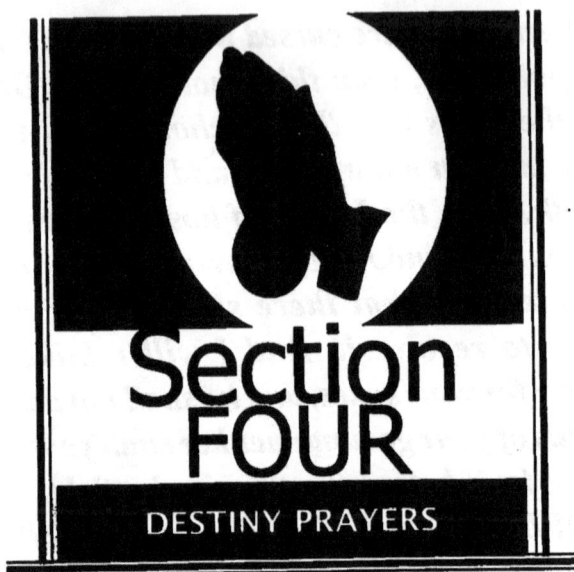

Section FOUR

DESTINY PRAYERS

Day 1

1. I release myself from every ancestral demonic pollution, in the name of Jesus.

2. I release myself from every inherited demonic pollution, in the name of. Jesus.

3. I release myself from every demonic pollution emanating from my past involvement in any demonic religion, in the name of Jesus.

4. 1 break and loose myself from every idol and related associations, in the name of Jesus.

5. I release myself from every dream pollution, in the name of Jesus.

6. Satanic attacks against my life in my dreams, be converted

to victory, in Jesus' name.

7.   Let all rivers, trees, forests, evil companions, evil pursuers, pictures of dead relatives, snakes, spirit husbands, spirit wives, and masquerades manipulated against me in the dream, be completely destroyed by the power in the blood of the Lord Jesus.

8.   I command every evil plantation in my life: Come out with all your roots, in the name of Jesus! (*Lay your hands on your stomach and keep repeating the emphasised area.*)

9.   I withdraw my health from the hands of the bondwoman and her children, in Jesus' name

10.   You bondwoman will not squander my divine opportunities, in the name of Jesus.

11.   I dismantle any power working against me, in the name of Jesus.

12.   I refuse to lock the door of blessing against myself, in the name of Jesus.

13.   I refuse to be a wandering star, in the name of Jesus.

14.   1 refuse to appear and disappear, in the name of Jesus.

15.   Let the riches of the gentiles, be transferred to me, in the name of Jesus.

16.   Angels of God, pursue every enemy of my prosperity to destruction, in Jesus' name.

17.   Let the sword of Goliath of poverty working against me die, in the name of Jesus.

18.   Let wealth change hands in my life, in the name of Jesus.

19.   Lord, make a hole in the roof of my house for my

prosperity, in the name of Jesus.

20. Let the yoke of poverty upon my life be dashed to pieces, in the name of Jesus.

21. Let every satanic siren scaring away my helpers be silenced, in the name of Jesus.

22. Let every masquerading power swallowing my prosperity be destroyed, in Jesus' name.

23. Let every coffin constructed against my prosperity, swallow the owner, in Jesus' name.

24. Let the ways of the evil angels of poverty delegated against me be dark and slippery, in the name of Jesus

25. Lord Jesus, hold my purse.

26. Every demonic scarcity, be dissolved by fire, in Jesus' name.

Day 2

1. Let every parental mistake affecting my life, be reversed, in the name of Jesus.
2. God, arise and let my hand be lifted up, in Jesus' name.
3. Every witchcraft- sponsored poverty, die, in Jesus' name.
4. Every altar of poverty in my place of birth, working against my prosperity, burn to ashes in Jesus' name.
5. Every satanic priest ministering against my prosperity on any evil altar, die by fire, in the name of Jesus.
6. Every strength and power of environmental altar, wishing poverty for my life, wither, in the name of Jesus.
7. Today, I raise the altar of continuous prosperity, upon my destiny, in the name of Jesus.
8. Every stronghold of physical and spiritual poverty in my life, be pulled down by fire, in the name of Jesus.
9. Any covenant in my life that is strengthening the stronghold of poverty, break, in the name of Jesus.
10. Every stronghold of poverty where I am living now and in my place of work, I pull you down, in Jesus' name
11. Lord, create opportunities for my prosperity today.
12. I bind and cast out every negative word enforcing poverty upon my life, in the name of Jesus.

Day 3

1. Spirit of stinginess, disappear from life, in Jesus name.
2. I bind and cast out the spirit of disobedience, in Jesus' name.
3. Where other people are spending money, I refuse to spend boldface, in the name of Jesus.
4. Every evil machinery against my prosperity, be destroyed, in the name of Jesus.
5. I destroy by fire every weapon of poverty targeted at my life, in name of Jesus.
6. Every descendant of poverty in my life, fall down and die, in the name of Jesus.
7. Every evil power, sitting on my prosperity, somersault and die, in the name of Jesus.
8. I break, every caldron of poverty, in Jesus' name.
9. You stronghold of poverty, receive the fire of God, in Jesus' name.
10. I cut my family and I off every inherited poverty, in the name of Jesus.
11. Every stigma of poverty in my life, be rubbed off by the blood of Jesus.
12. Every adjustment to humiliate me, I rebel against you, in the name of Jesus.
13. Every power adjusting my life to poverty, fall down and die, in the name of Jesus.
14. I shall not adjust to poverty, in the name of Jesus.

15. Holy Spirit, adjust my life to prosperity, in Jesus name.
16. You network chains of failure rattling my life, melt by fire, in the of Jesus.
17. You anchor of failure holding my destiny, break, in Jesus' name.
18. Every spiritual chain of slavery upon my life, break by fire, in the name of Jesus.
19. Every chain of inherited failure upon my life, break by fire, in the name of Jesus.
20. Let every evil seed of generational poverty dry up, in the name of Jesus.
21. I command the stronghold of inherited poverty in my life to be pulled down by the blood of Jesus.
22. Holy Ghost, arrest on my behalf every spirit of poverty, in the name of Jesus.
23. I dismantle every demonic opposition to my prosperity, in the name of Jesus.
24. Every satanic river of poverty and failure, dry up by fire, in the name of Jesus.
25. Every altar of poverty prepared by my ancestors, break now, in the name of Jesus.

DESTINY MARCHING ORDERS

YOU MUST MOVE FROM FOOLISHNESS TO WISDOM

Wisdom will accelerate your destiny while foolishness will slow down its progress. Wisdom is better than foolishness. To fulfill your destiny, you must get rid of actions that depict foolishness. Two people might be pursuing a similar destiny, but the wise will make it while the foolish will fail.

Proverb 8:11-12 says:

> *For wisdom is better than rubies; and all the things that may be desired are not to be compared to it. I wisdom dwell with prudence, and find out knowledge of witty inventions.*

Wisdom is the greatest instrument of destiny fulfillment. The wisdom of God has been from the ages. God's wisdom laid the foundation of the world. God Has continued to sustain the world through wisdom. If you really want your destiny to come out brilliantly, you must shun foolishness and embrace wisdom. You can only do this by acquiring the wisdom of God.

What is the wisdom of God? It is described in Proverb 8:14-35 which says:

> _Counsel is mine, and sound wisdom: I am understanding; I have strength. By me kings reign, and princes decree justice. By me princes rule, and nobles, even all the judges of the earth. I love them that love me; and those that seek me early shall find me. Riches and honour are with me; yea, durable riches and righteousness. My fruit is better than gold, yea, than fine gold; and my revenue than choice silver. I lead in the way of righteousness, in the midst of the paths of judgment: That I may cause those that love me to inherit substance; and I will fill their treasures. The LORD possessed me in the beginning of his way, before his works of old. I was set up from everlasting, from the beginning, or ever the earth was. When there were no depths, I was brought forth; when there were no fountains abounding with water. Before the mountains were settled,_

before the hills was I brought forth: While as yet he had not made the earth, nor the fields, nor the highest part of the dust of the world. When he prepared the heavens, I was there: when he set a compass upon the face of the depth: When he established the clouds above: when he strengthened the fountains of the deep: When he gave to the sea his decree, that the waters should not pass his commandment: when he appointed the foundations of the earth: Then I was by him, as one brought up with him: and I was daily his delight, rejoicing always before him; Rejoicing in the habitable part of his earth; and my delights were with the sons of men. Now therefore hearken unto me, O ye children: for blessed are they that keep my ways. Hear instruction, and be wise, and refuse it not. Blessed is the man that heareth me, watching daily at my gates, waiting at the posts of my doors. For whoso findeth me findeth life, and shall obtain favour of the LORD.

The passage above highlights the following qualities of wisdom.

1. Wisdom will give you counsel.
2. It will make you sound.
3. It will give you strength.
4. It will give you leadership qualities.

5. It will add value to your life.
6. It will give you riches and honour.
7. It will give you a glorious inheritance.
8. It will give you favour.
9. It will give you abundant life.
10. It will promote you.
11. It will place you on the express way of destiny fulfilment.

Section TWO

DESTINY CONFESSIONS

I am a product of divine wisdom. Foolishness is foreign to the realm of God. Wisdom dwells with God. By reason of my sonship connection with the spring of wisdom, I have lost the traces of folly. I have moved from foolishness to wisdom. I have said good bye to the thoughts of foolishness. I refuse to speak foolish words. I refuse to take foolish actions. I shall not keep the company of vain fellows. The trap of foolishness shall not catch me. The cage of foolishness shall not capture me. Wisdom has taken me out of the net of the fowler, and saved me from foolish, noisome pestilence.

I am climbing the mountain of wisdom. I am going higher in the school of wisdom. The wisdom of God has made me higher than my teachers. God's wisdom has rendered null and void the evil machinations of the wicked.

When the enemy comes against me with wicked craftsmanship, the wisdom of God shall give me victory. From now on, I shall go through the highway of wisdom to fulfill my destiny. I shall drink from the fountain of wisdom. I shall walk in wisdom. I shall abide in wisdom. I shall abound in wisdom.

Wisdom shall promote my destiny. It shall enable me to win the battles of life. It shall exhume my destiny from the grave of foolishness.

The anointing of wisdom shall fall upon me and I shall fulfill my destiny

The glory of God is as a covering round about me, in Jesus' name. In the name of Jesus Christ, I command the wicked to perish before me and melt away like wax. In the name of Jesus, none shall be able to stand before me all the days of my life. Amen.

I am built up in Christ Jesus. As Jesus is, so I am on the face of this earth, in the name of Jesus Christ. Amen.

I know who I am in Christ: I am a royal priesthood, I am a holy nation, I am a chosen generation and I am a peculiar person, delivered from the kingdom of darkness into the marvelous light of Christ Jesus, in Jesus' name. Amen.

I know who I am in Christ, in Jesus' name. Amen.

I am blood-washed. I am redeemed. I am justified by Christ. I am made to be the righteousness of God through Christ. I am a believer of the word of Truth. I am born again. I am heaven-bound: my citizenship is in heaven. I am seated with Christ in the heavenly places, far above principalities, powers and dominions. I am a priest and a king ordained by Christ to rule here on earth. I am the fear and the dread of God against the kingdom of darkness. I am a dwelling place of the Holy Spirit of God. I am built up together and attached with other children of God into a holy habitation of God. No power contrary to God's can change that. Amen.

The word of God says that I am a royal priesthood, I am a holy nation; I am a chosen generation and a peculiar person. I am special in the sight of God. The Bible says, because I believe and have received Jesus Christ, power has been given to me to become the son of God. I am empowered to trample upon serpents and scorpions and over all the power of the enemy. I am empowered to use the name of Jesus to cast out demons and heal the sick. I am empowered to bind, to loose and to decree things. The Bible says: that wherever my voice is heard no one can ask me why. I do these things for my voice is the voice of the king, full of authority.

Today, I begin to be what God says I am, and begin to walk in it, in the name of Jesus. I am a person of authority, power, dominion, grace and favour, in Jesus' name. I can run through a troop. I can leap over a wall. I can crush principalities and powers under my feet. I can pursue, overtake and break the necks of my enemies

I know the love of Christ which passeth knowledge, that I might be filled with all the fullness of God. Now, unto me shall God do exceeding abundantly above all that I ask, seek, desire and think, according to the power that He had made to work in me. The young lions do lack, and suffer hunger; but I who seek the Lord God Almighty shall not want any good thing. Promotion does not come form the north, south, east or west, it comes only from the Lord. And who is like unto our God, who dwells on high, far above all powers and dominions. He raiseth up the poor out of the dust and lifteth the needy out of the dunghill; that He might set him with princes. Even so shall the Lord do unto me.

I can do and possess all things through Christ who strengthens me. And my God shall supply all my need according to His riches in glory by Christ Jesus.

Christ has redeemed me from the curse of the law, being a curse for me in all His wealth, riches and opulence. He chose to be poor that I may be rich, and it is His divine and perfect will that I prosper in all things and above all things.

Section
THREE

DESTINY SCRIPTURES

I wisdom dwell with prudence, and find out knowledge of witty inventions. The fear of the LORD is to hate evil: pride, and arrogancy, and the evil way, and the froward mouth, do I hate. Counsel is mine, and sound wisdom: I am understanding; I have strength. By me kings reign, and princes decree justice. me princes rule, and nobles, even all the judges of the earth. I love them that love me; and those that seek me early shall find me. Riches and honour are with me; yea, durable riches and righteousness. My fruit is better than gold, yea, than fine gold; and my revenue than choice silver. I lead in the way of righteousness, in the midst of the paths of judgment: hat I may cause those that love me to inherit substance; and I will fill their treasures. The LORD possessed me in the beginning of his way, before his works of old. I was set up from everlasting, from the beginning, or ever the earth was. When there were no depths, I was brought forth; when there were no fountains abounding with water. Before the mountains were settled, before the hills was I brought forth: While as yet he had not made the earth, nor the fields, nor the highest part of the dust of the world. When he prepared the heavens, I was there: when he set a compass upon the face of the depth: When he established the clouds above: when he strengthened the fountains of the deep: When he gave to the sea his decree, that the waters should not pass his commandment: when he appointed the foundations of the earth: Then I was by him, as one brought up with him: and I was daily his delight, rejoicing always before him; Rejoicing in the habitable part of his earth; and my delights were with the sons of men. Now therefore hearken unto me, O ye children: for blessed are they that keep my ways. Hear instruction, and be wise, and refuse it not. Blessed is the man that heareth me, watching daily at my gates, waiting at the posts of my doors. For whoso findeth me findeth life, and shall obtain favour of the LORD. But he that sinneth against me wrongeth his own soul: all they that hate me love death. Prov 8:12-36.

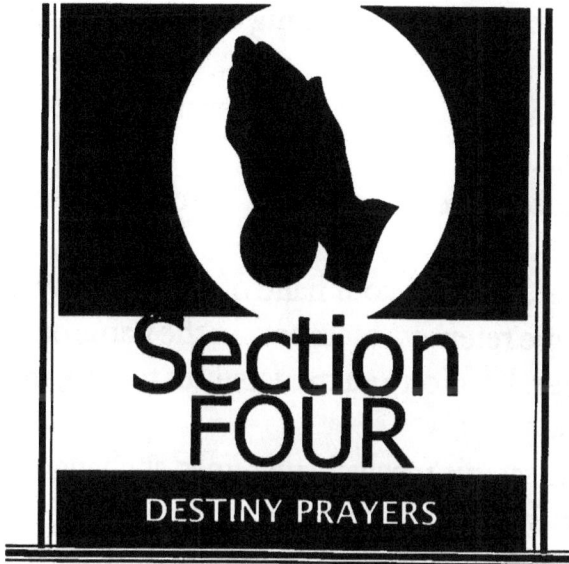

Section FOUR

DESTINY PRAYERS

Day 1

1.   I have more understanding than my teachers, because God's testimonies are my meditations, in the name of Jesus:
2.   Lord, give me understanding wisdom.
3.   Angels of the living God, encamp round about me now and go before me to the competition, in the name of Jesus.
4.   Father Lord, anoint my handiwork for success, in Jesus' name.
5.   I claim divine wisdom to answer any questions directed at me in the competition, in the name of Jesus.
6.   I excel my colleagues 10 times like Daniel, in Jesus' name
7.   I will find favour before the panel, in the name of Jesus.

8.   O Lord, perfect everything concerning my preparation for the competition.

9.   I bind and render to nothing every spirit of fear, in Jesus' name.

10. I release myself from every confusion and error, in the name of Jesus:

11. Father Lord, lay your hand of fire upon my memory and give me retentive memory, in the name of Jesus.

12. Father, I dedicate all my faculties to you, in the name of Jesus.

13. Let all satanic mechanisms aimed at changing my destiny be frustrated, in the name of Jesus.

14. Let all unprofitable broadcasters of my goodness, be silenced, in the name of Jesus.

15. Let every blessing confiscated by witchcraft spirits be released, in the name of Jesus.

16. Let every blessing confiscated by familiar spirits be released, in the name of Jesus.

17. Let every blessing confiscated by ancestral spirits be released, in the name of Jesus.

18. Let every blessing confiscated by envious enemies be released, in the name of Jesus.

19. Let every blessing confiscated by satanic agents be released, in the name of Jesus.

20. Let every blessing confiscated by principalities be released, in the name of Jesus.

21. Let every blessing confiscated by rulers of darkness be released, in the name of Jesus.

22.   Let every blessing confiscated by evil powers be released, in the name of Jesus.

23.   Let every blessing confiscated by spiritual wickedness in the heavenly places be released, in the name of Jesus.

24.   Let all demonic reverse gears installed to hinder my progress be roasted, in the name of Jesus.

25.   Anointing of the overcomer, fall upon me, in the name of Jesus.

26.   I claim my divine promotion today, in the name of Jesus.

27.   Thank God for answers to your prayers.

Day 2

1. I reject and denounce every spirit of failure, in Jesus' name.
2. I bind every spirit of financial failure, in the name of Jesus.
3. I break every curse of automatic failure working in my family, back to 10 generations on both sides of my family line, in the name of Jesus.
4. I break every curse of failure, in the name of Jesus.
5. Let all failures in the dream be converted to success, in Jesus' name.
6. I nullify all curses of failure in my life, in Jesus' name.
7. I pull down every stronghold of failure in my life, in Jesus' name.
8. I pull down every stronghold of failure in my marriage, in the name of Jesus.
9. I pull down every stronghold of failure in my business, in the name of Jesus.
10. Every pipeline of failure connected to my life, I command you to receive fire of God and be consumed, in Jesus' name.
11. Every spiritual barrier to success in my life, I command you to break into pieces, in the name of Jesus.
12. Every inherited and self-made failure in my life, I command you to receive repairs, in the name of Jesus.
13. Every seed of failure in my life, I command you to be

consumed by the fire of God, in the name of Jesus.

14. Every area of my life that I have lost to failure, I command you to be restored, in Jesus' name.

15. You spirit of failure, loose your grip over my life, in Jesus' name.

16. I refuse to register in the school of failure, in the mighty name of Jesus.

17. Lord, let me not enter the trap of failure.

18. I remove my name from the book of failure and demonic sidetrack, in the name of Jesus.

Day 3

1. I decree success, breakthroughs and progress into my handiwork, in the name of Jesus.
2. I decree happiness, peace and harmony into my handiwork, in the name of Jesus.
3. I destablise and paralyse all territorial spirits delegated against me, in the name of Jesus.
4. Let thunder and fire of God destroy every satanic monitoring device, in the name of Jesus.
5. I paralyse and destroy all satanic embargoes placed on my progress, in the name of Jesus.
6. Let all evil power seeking my destruction begin to turn against each other, in the name of Jesus.
7. Let all the havoc created by lack of patience in my life be repaired, in the name of Jesus.
8. Let all goodness withdrawn as a result of my being impatient be returned seven-fold, in the name of Jesus
9. Lord, remove every bitterness from my heart.
10. Spirit of the living God, fall afresh on me, in Jesus' name.
11. I command every part of my body to receive spiritual correction, in the name of Jesus.
12. I nullify all spiritual weapons being used to slow down my progress, in the name of Jesus.
13. I cancel all strongholds that the spirit of fear has built in me, in the name of Jesus.
14. Every witchcraft assemble in my neighbourhood, be

scattered by Holy Ghost fire, in the name of Jesus.

15. Let the stubborn strongman of poverty in my place of birth, (mention the place) be paralysed by fire, in the name of Jesus.

16. Every territorial spirit working against my prosperity, be chained, in the name of Jesus.

17. Every covenant made at my birth and in my place of birth, break, in the name of Jesus.

18. Every witchcraft covenant of poverty affecting my prosperity, break, in the name of Jesus.

19. Every covenant of poverty made by the living or dead against my prosperity, break, in the name of Jesus.

20. Hear, O heaven, I am dead to the covenant of poverty, I am alive to the covenant of prosperity, in the name of Jesus.

21. Every arrow of poverty fired into my life, come out with all your roots, in the name of Jesus.

22. Every curse of poverty placed upon my family, be consumed by fire, in the name of Jesus.

23. Every curse of poverty fired into my life by household wickedness, go back to your sender, in the name of Jesus.

24. As a result my prosperity prayers, I receive the mandate to enter into the covenants of wealth, in Jesus' name.

25. Lord, empower me to pluck the seed of wealth that will swallow poverty in my life.

DESTINY MARCHING ORDERS

YOU MUST MOVE FROM ENVYING OTHERS TO HELPING OTHERS

This is an uncommon marching order. You must move from the negative side of life to the positive side of life. You must not allow anything to make you concentrate on negative issues when there are positive issues to pursue. When you are struggling with envy, jealousy, pettiness and carnal sentiments, the journey of destiny will take longer than necessary.

If you see yourself below others, you will be busy envying them; but when you come up higher, you will begin to see yourself as someone on whom others depend on for survival. Consequently, you will give yourself to the task of serving others. Rather than dissipate energy on negative things, you will begin to pursue noble goals. Your thoughts and energy will be occupied with the virtues outlined in Philippians 4:8:

> *Finally, brethren, whatsoever things are true, whatsoever things are honest, whatsoever things are just, whatsoever things are pure, whatsoever things are lovely, whatsoever things are of good report; if there be any virtue, and if there be any praise, think on these things.*

You will move with maturity and speed when you get to the level where low and sordid aims are no longer attractive to you. The world is in need of men and women of destiny. You must address yourself to the issues of destiny. You must begin to serve others selflessly and faithfully. You must rescue the perishing and care for the dying. You must warm the lukewarm and arouse the complacent. You must help the helpless and clothe the naked. You must become eyes to the blind and legs to the lame. You must become a life line to those who appear beyond redemption. You must serve people far and near. You must become God's battle cry for your generation. May the Lord depend on you.

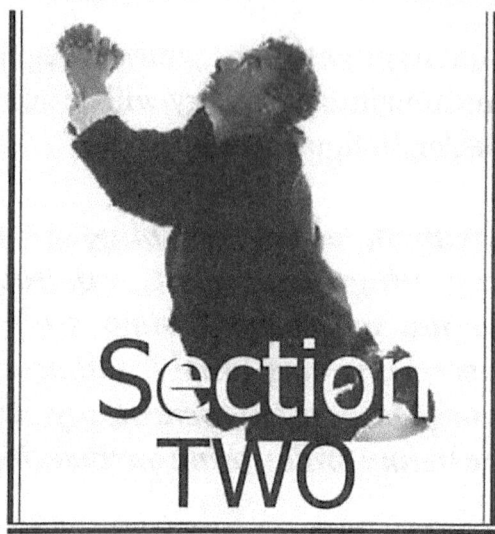

Section TWO

DESTINY CONFESSIONS

I am a child of God, a citizen of Heaven but a pilgrim on earth. The touch of God is upon my life. His hand is strong upon me and His influence is strong upon my destiny. I refuse to take up the character of the ungodly. The Lord has touched my heart and embossed my character with brokennes. Envy, malice, jealousy and all forms of pestilence are gone from my heart and life. I have moved from envying others to helping others. God has placed me on the platform of godliness.

He has purged me of all carnal sentiments. Self has been buried and I am now risen with Christ. While others are living in envy and jealousy, I have moved forward. I am no longer part of the company of those who are involved with backbiting and putting others down. God has built my destiny and converted me to a builder of destiny.

My mission on earth is not to envy but to help others. I am a helper of destiny. My resolve is to go about like my Lord and Master, Jesus Christ, doing good and helping people. I am a pillar in the household of faith, not a caterpillar.

I am a helper not a destroyer. I am a specialist in building up, not in pulling down. The devil shall not give me an assignment. The devil shall not succeed in bringing up carnal uprisings in my heart. Helping others, is one of the cardinal points of my destiny. Nothing will evoke envy or jealousy within me.

Jesus is the Captain of my heart. He is my ruler and my Controller. I have therefore surrendered my heart to Him. The King of kings lives with me. Therefore, envy and jealousy have packed their baggage and departed. I shall grow in grace, long suffering, tender companionship and in sacrificial services to all who need my help.

My God is with me, whom shall I be afraid of. He that spared not His own Son, but delivered him up for us all, how shall He not with Him also freely give me all things? Who shall lay anything to the charge of God's elect? I am God's elect and He alone justifies. Who is he that condemns? Is it Christ that died, yea rather, that is risen again, Who is even at the right hand of

God, who also maketh intercessions for me? He also shall fight my own battles.

The Lord shall pass through Judah; He shall overflow and go over. He shall reach even to the neck, and the stretching out of His wings shall fill the breadth of my land, O Immanuel. Associate yourselves, O ye people, and ye shall be broken in pieces, and give ear all ye of far countries; gird yourselves, and ye shall be broken in pieces. Take counsel together and it shall come to nought; speak the word, and it shall not stand; for God is with me.

The Lord is my light and my salvation, whom shall I fear? The Lord is the strength of my life; of whom shall I be afraid? When the wicked, even my enemies and foes, come upon me to eat up my flesh, they stumbled and fell.

The Lord, God, my God, will help me; therefore shall I not be confounded: therefore have I set my face like a flint, and I know that I shall not be ashamed. It is written: "Behold, I lay in Zion a stumbling stone and a rock of offence: and whosoever believeth on Him shall not be ashamed. My God, the Father of Jesus Christ, is with me as a mighty terrible One: therefore my persecutors shall stumble, and they shall not prevail: they shall be greatly ashamed: for they shall not prevail over you.

Section
THREE

DESTINY SCRIPTURES

Who hath believed our report? and to whom is the arm of the LORD revealed? For he shall grow up before him as a tender plant, and as a root out of a dry ground: he hath no form nor comeliness; and when we shall see him, there is no beauty that we should desire him. He is despised and rejected of men; a man of sorrows, and acquainted with grief: and we hid as it were our faces from him; he was despised, and we esteemed him not. Surely he hath borne our griefs, and carried our sorrows: yet we did esteem him stricken, smitten of God, and afflicted. But he was wounded for our transgressions, he was bruised for our iniquities: the chastisement of our peace was upon him; and with his stripes we are healed. All we like sheep have gone astray; we have turned every one to his own way; and the LORD hath laid on him the iniquity of us all. He was oppressed, and he was afflicted, yet he opened not his mouth: he is brought as a lamb to the slaughter, and as a sheep before her shearers is dumb, so he openeth not his mouth. He was taken from prison and from judgment: and who shall declare his generation? for he was cut off out of the land of the living: for the transgression of my people was he stricken. And he made his grave with the wicked, and with the rich in his death; because he had done no violence, neither was any deceit in his mouth. Yet it pleased the LORD to bruise him; he hath put him to grief: when thou shalt make his soul an offering for sin, he shall see his seed, he shall prolong his days, and the pleasure of the LORD shall prosper in his hand. He shall see of the travail of his soul, and shall be satisfied: by his knowledge shall my righteous servant justify many; for he shall bear their iniquities. Therefore will I divide him a portion with the great, and he shall divide the spoil with the strong; because he hath poured out his soul unto death: and he was numbered with the transgressors; and he bare the sin of many, and made intercession for the transgressors. Isa 53:1-12.

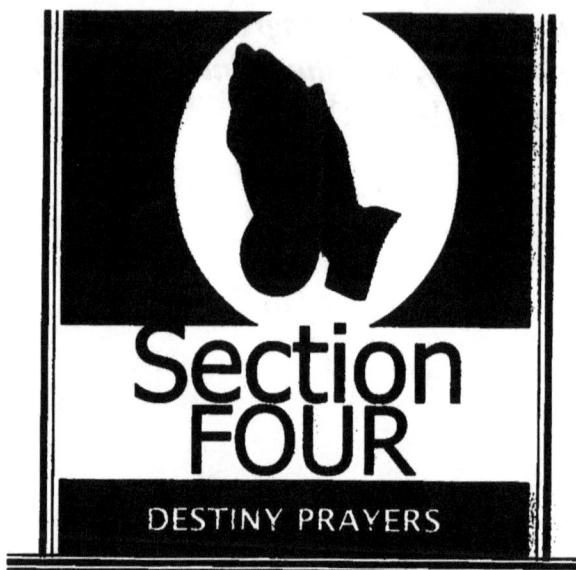

Section FOUR

DESTINY PRAYERS

Day 1

1. Holy Ghost fire, arise and damage every resistance to the glow of my star, in the name of Jesus.
2. Thou star demoters, receive the sword of fire, in Jesus' name.
3. I recover my star from the cage of star hunters, in Jesus' name.
4. I rise above every dark sentence issued against my star, in the name of Jesus.
5. Let the pattern of darkness be broken to pieces, in Jesus' name.
6. I put to flight, every organised warfare against my star, in the name of Jesus.

7. Every pit dug to swallow my star, be covered by the blood of Jesus.

8. Let the star of my destiny pick fire and overtake its contemporaries, in the name of Jesus.

9. Every evil wise man observing the star of my destiny, receive blindness, in the name of Jesus.

10. Every power of the valley, die, in the name of Jesus.

11. I destroy every spell and jinx placed upon my star, in Jesus' name.

12. Let the power of God move me forward by fire, in Jesus' name.

Day 2

1. Fire of God, minister destruction to the ministry of destruction in my family, in the name of Jesus.
2. I consume the shrine of the strongman in my family with the fire of God, in the name of Jesus.
3. Let stones of fire pursue and dominate all the strongmen in my life, in the name of Jesus.
4. I receive strength and power to be a warrior and not to worry, in the name of Jesus.
5. I smash the head of the strongman on the wall of fire, in the name of Jesus.
6. Let hell open its mouth without measure and swallow all suckers of peace in my life, in the name of Jesus.
7. There shall be no regrouping and no reinforcement against me by the strongmen in my family, in the name of Jesus.
8. Let the angels of God roll in the stones of fire to hinder the strongman on my ways, in the name of Jesus.
9. I cause open disgrace to all strongmen in my family, in Jesus' name.
10. Let all the enemies of my soul start their days in confusion and end it in destruction, in the name of Jesus.
11. Lord, release from my mind any image of jealousy, lust and evil intentions.
12. I stand against all confusing forces within me, in Jesus' name.

13. Lord, order my inner life so that I can hear you.

14. I ask You, O Lord, to make me uncomfortable till I get on the right track.

15. Lord, wash my brain with the blood of Jesus and remove bad habits which are physically engraved there.

16. Lord, heal any hormonal imbalance or other unwanted secretions in my body.

17. Lord, heal me in whatever needs to be healed.

18. Lord, replace in me whatever needs to be replaced.

19. Lord, transform me in whatever needs to be transformed.

20. Lord, let your healing power take firm root within me.

21. Let the strongmen from both sides of my family destroy themselves now, in the name of Jesus.

22. The strongman from my father's side, the strongman from my mother's side, destroy yourselves, in the name of Jesus.

23. I refuse to wear the garment of sorrow, in the name of Jesus.

24. All stubborn pursuers in my life, I command you to die, in the name of Jesus.

Day 3

1. All satanic arrows presently in my life, lose your power, in the name of Jesus.
2. Let every organised evil arrow against my life be paralysed, in the name of Jesus.
3. I fire back all satanic arrows of depression at the edge of my breakthroughs, in the name of Jesus.
4. I fire back all satanic arrows of spiritual and physical sicknesses, in the name of Jesus.
5. I fire back all satanic arrows of weakness in my prayers and Bible reading, in the name of Jesus.
6. I fire back all satanic arrows of business failure, in Jesus' name.
7. I fire back all evil arrows from the household enemy, in the name of Jesus.
8. I fire back all evil arrows from my unfriendly friends, in Jesus' name.
9. Power of God, bring to life all my good benefits that satanic arrows have paralysed, in the name of Jesus
10. I cover my life and all my belongings from satanic arrows the blood of Jesus.
11. Thank the Lord that the gates of hell shall not prevail against your life.
12. I order confusion of tongues against all wicked associations militating against the peace of my life, in Jesus' name.

287 Marching Orders to Fulfil Your Destiny

13. Let the wisdom of all evil counsellors in my life be rendered to nothing, in the name of Jesus.
14. Lord, cause an explosion of your power in my handiwork.
15. O Lord, let my life be barricaded by the edge of fire and let me be soaked and covered with the blood of Jesus
16. Lord, smite at the cheekbones all evil tongues and mouths rising against me and break the jaws of evil.
17. Let every handwriting contrary to my peace receive intensive disgrace, in the name of Jesus.
18. Let every decision taken against me by the wicked be rendered null and void, in the name of Jesus.

OTHER BOOKS BY DR. D. K. OLUKOYA

YORUBA PUBLICATIONS

1   ADURA AGBAYORI
2   ADURA TI NSI OKE NIDI
3   OJO ADURA

FRENCH PUBLICATIONS

1   PLUIE DE PRIERE
2   ESPIRIT DE VAGABONDAGE
3   EN FINIR AVEC LES FORCES MALEFIQUES DE LA
     MAISON DE TON PERE
4   QUE I'ENVOUTEMENT PERISSE
5   FRAPPEZ I'ADVERSAIRE ET IL FUIRA
6   COMMENT RECEVIOR LA DELIVRANCE DU MARI ET
     FEMME DE NUIT
7   CPMMENT SE DELIVRER SOI-MEME
8   POVOIR CONTRE LES TERRORITES SPIRITUEL
9   PRIERE DE PERCEES POUR LES HOMMES D'AFFAIRES
10   PRIER JUSQU'A REMPORTER LA VICTOIRE
11   PRIERES VIOLENTES POUR HUMILIER LES
     PROBLEMES OPINIATRES
12   PRIERE POUR DETRUIRE LES MALADIES ET
     INFIRMITES
13   LE COMBAT SPIRITUEL ET LE FOYER
14   BILAN SPIRITUEL PERSONNEL
15   VICTOIRES SUR LES REVES SATANIQUES
16   PRIERES DE COMAT CONTRE 70 ESPIRITS

ANNUAL 70 DAYS PRAYER AND FASTING PUBLICATIONS

www.ingramcontent.com/pod-product-compliance
Lightning Source LLC
Chambersburg PA
CBHW062151080426
42734CB00010B/1652